TOWARD THE
GREAT AWAKENING

Sidney W. Powell

ABINGDON-COKESBURY PRESS

New York ● *Nashville*

TOWARD THE GREAT AWAKENING

SET UP, PRINTED, AND BOUND BY THE
PARTHENON PRESS, AT NASHVILLE,
TENNESSEE, UNITED STATES OF AMERICA

Contents

I

The Lost Capstone

CONSTERNATION REIGNED. The builders had carried the main arch of the temple to completion except for a gapping space at its otherwise majestic summit. It stood like a ruined work of art, with a ghastly rent where the lovely central figure should have imparted meaning to the whole. Now the workmen were in a dither, for the arch must remain incomplete until they could discover a single stone of unusual shape to fit into this open space. Perplexed and confused, they rushed about, carefully measuring each of the stones that lay in great heaps around the building, but none was found that would fit. They had been cut at the quarries many miles away. Each was marked for its particular place, and the workmen laid them up without the sound of a hammer in all the building of the temple.

After long and frantic search, in a pile of rubbish now overgrown with brush and weeds, the workmen found a curiously cut stone unlike the others. It was neither oblong nor square. When this particular stone had been delivered to the builders they had looked at it, measured it, and, because it was apparently a misfit, they had thrown it aside as unusable and gone on with their work. Now they brought it from the rubbish heap and lifted it to the eloquent space at the top of the arch. To their surprise and satisfaction it fit perfectly, and the arch stood complete.

This ancient legend is probably the foundation for the oft-repeated passage of scripture: "The stone which the builders rejected, the same is become the head of the corner." This scripture has been variously applied. Our Lord related it to himself. "He is despised and rejected of men," yet in the first Pentecostal sermon Peter was able to assert with boldness, "God hath made that same Jesus, whom ye have crucified,

7

both Lord and Christ." "This is the Lord's doing, and it is marvelous in our eyes."

In a seminar held at a leading American university a few years ago a prominent educator said to some three hundred public-school teachers, "We must rebuild the world apart from the spiritual." By and large that has been the attitude not only of educators but of the common man as well in present-day United States. But the spiritual is the essential capstone of all life. The arch of modern life is tottering and threatening to collapse because this capstone is not in its intended place. Every major transition in human history has been steadied by a spiritual awakening that preserved the new forms of life from the dangers incident to revolutionary changes. When Charlemagne's empire fell and Europe was threatened with a return to barbarism, the feudal system sprang up. But at the close of the twelfth century this system was at the point of collapse. At the same time the papal system, which had gained absolute sway over western Europe, was being challenged both by the growing power of secular authorities and by the growing intelligence of the people. An epoch was drawing to a close. Painfully new ideas, new ways, new forms of life were being born, for which the men of that day were ill-prepared. They might have produced chaos had it not been that at that particular moment in human history there appeared that troubadour of God, Francis of Assisi, who launched a vast spiritual movement which saved men from the grave dangers and uncertainties of the hour.

In the sixteenth century, men who had left the feudal castles of their protectors to dwell in cities drew together in the larger organizations of nations. Kings were beginning to exercise enormous new powers, while at the same time there arose a fresh demand for freedom on the part of the populace. Again a door was being opened upon innovations fraught with grave dangers. Delivered from the harsh restraints of Romanism, the only religion widely known in Europe in that day, the new freedom might easily have developed into anarchy, and man's escape from these rigid religious restraints might have ended in atheism had there not emerged a new concept of religion based upon the Word of God and its demands for godly living. The Reformation released a redeeming Christ from the cerements of sacerdotalism, the obscurations of gross misrepresentation, the fetters of a church that claimed him as its exclusive possession, along with the Holy Scriptures and the keys to the Kingdom of Heaven. As he had come from the tomb in his glorious resurrection, so he came forth from the church, where he had been hidden, as in another tomb, and men saw him as a gracious Redeemer, freely offering them the benefit of divine grace on the basis of simple faith, without money and without price. The Bible became the people's book. In it they read the magna charta of their liberties. The church was reclaimed from the arrogant clergy and again became an institution of the people as it had been in New Testament times. Thus another vast transition in human life was given spiritual direction.

In England, at the beginning of the eighteenth century, new ways of life brought the land close to bloody revolution. The age of machinery, the rise of the manufacturing classes, threatened chaos and disintegration. Then the great evangelical awakening under John Wesley lifted the keystone of faith to its proper place and thus steadied the arch of national life. It is hard to believe that these times of spiritual awakening coincided with periods of change and transition by mere historic happenstance.

In our day the world is entering the most dangerous and alarming period man has ever known. Even the political economists and the scientists, who are largely responsible for the new age, are turning in fear to the church, begging her to invoke the spiritual power to which she has access, to control the appalling means of human annihilation which have been created. The twentieth century stands in more desperate need of a spiritual awakening than any of those sister centuries which escaped doom through revival.

Born out of a great revival of religion, her foundations laid in spirituality, the United States can maintain herself and fulfill her destiny only by adhering to the principles and purposes of those early architects who laid her foundations, and that Architect from whom they learned their political and social strategy.

The word "revival" has of late fallen into disrepute. Not a few among us pronounce the word "evangelism" with thinly veiled contempt. In his book *Evangelism in the Home Church* Andrew W. Blackwood calls attention to the significant fact that when Henry Ward Beecher delivered the first three series of the Lyman Beecher Lectures on preaching at Yale he devoted considerable time to the subject of revivals. Phillips Brooks, Robert W. Dale, and Bishop Matthew Simpson emphasized evangelism. But with the beginning of a new century there was a marked change. The emphasis was placed upon social problems, although evangelism was also considered. Since 1918, Blackwood notes, there has been little mention of evangelism in the Yale lectures. It no longer seems to be a vital emphasis in the church generally. Yet an adequate evangelism, including in it all that Jesus intended, is the cornerstone of Christianity upon which the whole structure depends. An Oriental writer tells us that in his country when a person plans to build a house first he gathers the stones for the structure. Then he hires laborers to do the building. The laborers inspect the stones and uniformly reject the largest ones because it will be hard to lift them to their places. The employer, however, insists that these stones be used. After considerable debate the workmen agree to use the larger stones in the foundation, and they place the largest one in the corner. A true and worthy evangelism is not a small decorative stone in the building, like the showy but superficial emotionalism that too frequently parades as evangelism; it is the chief cornerstone of evangelical Christianity. Someone has said that the strongest argument in favor of evangelism is that there is no substitute for it. Nothing can take its place. Evangelicalism without evangelism is like an automobile without an engine—the thing that makes it go. Without evangelism a church may perpetuate a tradition, preserve a ritual, accumulate wealth, attract attendance, but the lack of the vitamins essential to its health will eventually cause its death. Its name may live but in reality it is dead.

Yet to assert that evangelism has been completely neglected by the majority of present-day churches would be too sweeping a generalization without basis in fact. The 404-foot spire of Salisbury Cathedral, built in 1250, and famous in literature and art, was recently pronounced to be in perilous condition, not because the cornerstone had been removed but because the lofty spire has moved two feet off center.

No ecclesiastical pronouncement has ever banned evangelism, but little by little in course of time, buffeted by the brash winds of modernity, pressed by the secularities of new thought, while the custodians have not been too attentive to its foundations, almost imperceptibly the church has moved off center. To be sure, its present perilous condition is attributed to many things, but not inconspicuous among them is the fact that it has moved the center of emphasis from evangelism to other worthy but less essential considerations. At a summer conference a minister, by many standards considered a success, admitted to me: "I have been program-conscious. My programs have generally succeeded but I have stopped short of winning men for Christ." If churches were as honest as that minister, many of them would have to own up to the same fatal weakness. Some of them are in perilous condition because the capstone has been removed. More are endangered because their emphasis is off center. It is not sufficient for the purposes of his art that an author have merely a hazy idea of his theme. It must ever be held sharply and clearly in his mind else he will sacrifice force and coherence in his production. It is equally essential that the church shall hold in mind the exact purpose of its Founder. Jesus said: "Therefore whosoever heareth these sayings of mine, and doeth them, I will liken him unto a wise man, which built his house upon a rock. . . . And every one that heareth these sayings of mine, and doeth them not, shall be likened unto a foolish man, which built his house upon the sand: and the rain descended, and the floods came, and the

11

winds blew, and beat upon that house; and it fell: and great was the fall of it."

Faithfully observing his own teaching, when Jesus began to build his own house he established it upon a rock. "Upon this rock," said he, "I will build my church; and the gates of hell shall not prevail against it." That rock was the achievement of personal faith in him. The church is not an end in itself. It is an organization with a clearly defined purpose, that purpose being to win men to Christ and to build them up in our most holy faith. It is essential to hold the plumb line against the church frequently enough to make certain that it stands firmly on its foundation. Almost every church in the denomination to which I belong would resent an implication that it is not evangelistic. Incensed defenders would promptly rise to insist that "our church has always been evangelistic"; but careful study of almost any church, and the organizations of which it is made up, would doubtless produce startling surprises as it did in a church of some four thousand members in a Pacific Coast city. One would consider a church that received 250 new members on profession of faith in a year an evangelistic church, but when 250 members of this particular church, representing its seventy-one organizations, sat down together to evaluate the service of their organizations, they were shocked to discover that they were not even beginning to reach their own constituency. Among others, they asked themselves these questions: "Are we winning for Christ the people who give us a chance? Are we visiting them with the purpose of winning them? Do we know in particular those whom we should win, or do we know them just in a general way? Do we have the proper sort of responsibility lists?"

When they had completed their study, and the facts were laid before the group, the pastor said: "I never realized before how little we are doing compared with what we should be doing. We have a great social program in our church and its organizations. In fact we have everything but evangelism in this supposedly evangelistic church. We have received 250 people a year on profession of faith when we should have been

12

receiving 400 a year. This must not continue. It is going to be changed."

Many churches would do well to increase the drawing power of their social life and lay greater emphasis upon Christian fellowship, but to dally with the fatuous dream that the church can be floated to port on a social sea of tepid tea is to court shipwreck—the sinking of our craft in the sea of oblivion. If socials alone do not serve to bring success to the church neither will social service.

Says Paul Scherer in his book *For We Have This Treasure:*

Policies and programs are not of the same order as salvation: they are quite capable of turning out to be its contradictions. They are the issue of redemption; they are not the road to it. They are the feet of religion; but when religion is carried out feet first, it is dead. There is forever something inside that has to happen, lest there be either no desire or the wrong motive or method. We have to come to grips with God by way of "personal encounter"; even as we come to grips with the world. Then shall we hold in our hands a redeeming transforming power.

.   .   , ...

I have no enthusiasm for any attempt to clean up my street by first hanging pictures on the walls of every apartment and repairing the wash basins, though all this may have to be done. I am saving my first enthusiasm—not so much in point of time as in point of importance—for the attempt to go straight to the middle of things and change men and women; after which both the art and the plumbing presumably will come in for some improvement.[1]

Evangelism means confronting people with the claims of Christ and the gospel. It is such a presentation of Christ as will lead men to accept him as Lord and Saviour. It is related to the program of the Christian church as harvesting is related to farming. Harvesting is not all there is to farming, but it is the major purpose of all that is done on the farm. The farmer prepares the soil, plants the seed, cultivates the young plants, with his eye always upon the harvest which is to come. Just

[1] By permission of Harper & Brothers.

13

so, evangelism is not the whole Christian program, but it should be the major purpose of all the workers all the time to bring people to Christ and to produce full-grown souls in Christ. The harvest is the farmer's fortune. To plant and culti-vate through long days of arduous toil and then to abandon the farm with fields waving with golden grain would be the height of ridiculousness.

Evangelism is the climax of all Christian endeavor. It is the reward for long days and years of preparation. Some churches sow but they do not reap, or, to return to the former figure of speech, they have been moved ever so slightly, but none the less disastrously, off center. In them evangelism has suffered by adulteration. Its function has been obscured by those who want to include in it everything in the church's program. They rise up on every side saying, "Lo, this is evangelism. Let us put this in," until evangelism becomes a sort of ecclesiastical rag bag into which we stuff all sorts of things until it loses all shape and form. We must be jealous for evangelism at this point lest, as George Eliot says, "like an omnibus, we take on board anybody and anything which beckons as we pass." When we do that the impact of evangelism is negligible. There is of course, on the other hand, the danger of narrowing our conception of evangelism to the point where it becomes so circumscribed that it is a weak and unworthy servant of the gospel of Christ. The thought of evangelism is repulsive to some Christians because it suggests high-pressure emotional appeals, narrowness, intolerance, and crudity.

Evangelism is like a church window, as dark and unillu-mined as a piece of slate when there is no light behind it. Unillumined by reverent devotion, gracious culture, and an appreciation of the depth and height and breadth of Chris-tianity, evangelism may be offensive to fine Christian sensibility. But a new day dawns, new content is brought into evangelism, and all the color, warmth, and glow of the gospel returns to make it a thing of beauty and power.

Though at times rejected by the builders, the building is weakened without this capstone, and will in time collapse.

14

Returning from England a number of years ago, the late President E. Y. Mullins, of the Southern Baptist Theological Seminary, told of the ground being lost by the Nonconformist churches of the British Isles: "If I should sum up the cause in one word, it is because the pastors and the churches in that country have lost the power to convert people. What we need and must get is the divine power to change the human heart."

Horatius Bonar once said: "Ministers are seldom honored with success unless they are continually aiming at the conversion of sinners." Years ago a Boston pastor reported: "Under Whitefield's preaching more people came to me in one week in deep concern about their souls than in the whole twenty-four years of my ministry."

The church has made its greatest progress in those vast waves of sensibility that have from time to time swept over countries, nations, and sometimes the whole world. These tides of evangelism have also brought national deliverance as, by way of example, they brought it to England. Voltaire had received his "philosophy of nature and humanism" from the smart set in England and transplanted it to the soil of France. The result was the Reign of Terror. France had thrown off the restraints of religion and crowned a prostitute Goddess of Reason; the gutters of Paris ran with human blood and "each new champion of freedom, crying 'Liberty, Equality, and Fraternity,' rushed his fellow champions to the guillotine, lest they rush him there first."

Frederick the Great brought Voltaire from France to Germany, where the philosopher joined the court of his patron. Voltaire carried the roots of his philosophy from France to plant them in the fertile soil of Germany, and the tares of humanism choked the growing wheat of Christianity. Other husbandmen of the tares followed Voltaire. Nietzsche further developed his philosophy, adding to it his own doctrines of "the will to power," "the superman," "the overlord state." Nietzsche's product was consumed by the German people like a tasty new breakfast food. Presently a man stood up in Germany and said in effect: "Germany is strong with the 'will to

15

power.' I will be the supreme 'superman' and Germany the 'overlord state.'" And today Germany lies in ashes, and the glory that was Berlin is no more.

A searching question arises. If the "materialism" and "humanism" of England, carried to France, produced the Reign of Terror, and transported to Germany in time brought the destruction of that great country, why did it not destroy England, the place from whence it came? That was

the England of the slave-trader, the kidnapper, the smuggler; the England of trading-justices, South Sea Bubbles and commercial cupidity; the England of gin-shops, sodden ignorance and incredible child neglect; the England of bestial sports, mad gambling and parading wantonness. It was the England of corrupt politics and soulless religion: the England of "materialism," "dim ideals" and "expiring hopes,"

the England in which Montesquieu said there "was no such thing as religion," and where "if anyone spoke of it everybody laughed." In his *History of England* Smollett says of the early eighteenth century: "Thieves and robbers were now become more desperate and savage than they had ever appeared since mankind was civilized." Footpads armed with "bludgeons," pistols, cutlasses," infested "not only private lanes and passages, but likewise public streets and places of usual concourse," committing dastardly outrages even at time of day "hitherto deemed hours of security." England was "headed for chaos and disintegration." In those days Bishop Berkeley wrote:

Morality and religion have collapsed to a degree that has never been known in any Christian country! Our prospect is very terrible, and the symptoms grow worse from day to day. The accumulating torrent of evil, which threatens a general inundation and destruction of these realms [may be attributed chiefly to] the irreligion and bad example of those—styled the better sort. . . . The youth born and brought up in wicked times without any bias to good from early principle, or instilled opinion when they grow ripe must be monsters indeed, and it is to be feared that the age of monsters is not far off.

16

Then it was that a priest of the Church of England, after experiencing bitter failure in his sacerdotal ministry, was genuinely converted. He began to preach the simple gospel from the New Testament to his countrymen. His countrymen heeded, and a whole nation "headed for chaos and disintegration" turned around and began the greatest period of expansion in her history.

J. R. Green, the historian, claims that the revival under John Wesley "changed after a time the whole tone of English society."

The church was restored to new life and activity. Religion carried to the hearts of the people a fresh spirit of moral zeal, while it purified our literature and our manners. A new philanthropy reformed our prisons, infused clemency and wisdom into our penal laws, abolished the slave trade, and gave the first impulse to popular education.

Lecky avers that the evangelicals gradually

changed the whole spirit of the English Church. They infused into it a new fire and passion of devotion, kindled a spirit of fervent philanthropy, raised the standard of clerical duty, and completely altered the whole tone and tendency of the preaching of its ministers.

Overton writes:

Of the faith which enabled a man to abandon the cherished habits of a lifetime, and to go forth ready to spend and be spent in his Master's service, . . . which made the selfish man self-denying, the discontented happy, the worldling spiritually-minded, the drunkard sober, the sensual chaste, the liar truthful, the thief honest, the proud humble, the godless godly, the thriftless thrifty—we can only judge by the fruits which it bore. That such fruits were borne is surely undeniable.

Twentieth-century America is in many respects very like eighteenth-century England. What happened in the latter

17

country, amid the great transition taking place in that day, can happen here in the greater transition taking place among us today, and nothing but a genuine, all-pervading revival of spiritual religion can bring it about. A revival can change the whole tenor of American life, and it can do it in a remarkably short time. It took only a generation to militarize Japan and about ten years to nazify Germany. When a revival begins it may spread with the rapidity of a forest fire.

II

Ebb and Flow

A FIVE-YEAR-OLD BOY saw the ocean for the first time, A. C. Archibald tells us in his book *New Testament Evangelism*. With his pail and shovel clutched in his hand, he stood looking at the waves breaking on the shore. When next morning he came to the beach for his first dip in the sea the tide was out. A long stretch of yellow sand lay between him and the water. The child turned away in disappointment. "Will it ever come back?" he asked. A few hours later the tide had come in. Gleefully he jumped up and down.

"Daddy, does it always come back like that after it has gone out?"

"Always, my son," was the father's answer.

Modern Christians ask the boy's question: "Does it always come back?" Or, looking upon a moribund society, a pagan civilization, slumbering churches, with lifeless sermons droned in dead pulpits, they ask the question of an ancient prophet: "Can these bones live?"

You have perhaps driven through the passes of the Rockies and noticed that often for long stretches the snow-capped peaks are obscured by lower foothills. Then suddenly the lofty summits emerge in all their pristine glory. Or, in an airplane you have zoomed down cloud canyons so deep and thick it seemed there could be no sun in the heavens, and then in a split second the plane came out of the celestial canyon and the sun burst into full view above blue-white clouds with salmon-pink draperies over the western horizon. So it is with evangelism. It is obscured for a time, uninspired, the beauty departed; then of a sudden there is a recrudescence of its beauty and irresistible force.

There is a historic rhythm in evangelism. The tide ebbs and

flows. In an old history, now out of print, the author describes a cycle of evangelism descending from spiritual fervor to a growing lack of enthusiasm in the Lord's work. This in time develops into indifference, even creeping into the pulpit, followed by neglect of the cardinal doctrines of the Word of God, then the lowest point in the cycle, actual denial of the cardinal doctrines of the faith. When the church comes to this lowest state a reaction sets in and the way is prepared for a new spiritual awakening. Pentecost has been repeated time after time in the history of the church; yet nonetheless the tide often went out and remained out for long periods during which the church languished. Still it is always when the tide is farthest out that it is most ready to turn and come in again. It is when the night is darkest that light is nearest birth. It is when the world sinks to its lowest level, and Christians are painfully conscious of their complete inadequacy for their impossible task, that in their bewilderment and limitation they throw themselves upon God. Then comes the miracle of new birth and revival. It is at Gethsemane that Christ meets our anguish with his atoning blood. Ambrose Bailey says: "There has been no single century of Christian history when some significant outpouring of divine grace has not occurred." Different means have been employed, and different emphases have been made, but flood tide has always followed ebb tide.

Soon after the close of the apostolic period a black night of formalism and sacerdotalism settled over the church. Yet eventually the tide turned in the time of Wycliffe, John Huss, Calvin, and Luther. During the Protestant Reformation tens of thousands were converted in Germany, Switzerland, France, Holland, Great Britain, and Scandinavia. The church was delivered from sacerdotalism, and a religion of pious but empty forms. Persecution of the reformers was swallowed up in the tidal wave of the spirit, and opposition fell back exhausted and helpless like a man trying to stem the impervious tide while the tide continued to rise to greater heights. Though still in the University of Prague, John Huss received the prophet's mantle that fell from the shoulders of Wycliffe. He proclaimed the Scriptures with such power that his whole land was filled with a knowledge of the word of God. Savonarola, in Italy, fought the corruption and paganism of his city of Florence, and at the same time denounced the abuses of an apostate church. While Savonarola still waged his relentless fight for pure religion, Martin Luther in Germany threw off the superstition and corruption of Romanism, and in spite of all the threats of the hierarchy continued to strike telling blows against evil, and at the same time to build securely a structure of pure and undefiled religion. Under John Calvin the revival broke out in Switzerland. John Knox took up the torch in Scotland and started in every glen of that bonnie land fires that no man or devil could extinguish. Under his cyclonic influence the whole church of Scotland was brought into newness of life.

Thus was the church in Europe awakened from its long sleep of centuries. The capstone of the rounded arch was again lifted to the place it had occupied in the early church. The church was restored to its normal life in Christ, and aroused to its privilege of winning men for its Lord. Wishart, Cooper, and Welsh continued in such power the work begun by Knox in Scotland that the whole land was moved toward God. By the latter part of the seventeenth and the early part of the eighteenth century, however, the tide which had reached its crest in the Reformation had run out. The world, unwashed by any wave of evangelism, again revealed the ugly reefs and bars of corruption, degeneracy, and profligacy; again the light of spirituality burned low in the church. Conversion was rare and piety seemed almost dead. But again, under John Wesley, a new spiritual awakening was inaugurated in England, and wave after wave of spiritual influence rose, each higher than the one that had preceded it, until England was cleansed and lifted to new heights.

In 1734 the revival spread to America, and while the waters still rose to greater flood throughout England, Scotland, and Ireland, all the American colonies were visited with refreshment from on high. In 1739 Whitefield came to America. He preached in the fields to throngs of twenty and thirty thousand people.

Thousands were won for Christ. Historians have estimated that from twenty-five to fifty thousand were added to the churches of New England in consequence of the revival.

Then again the tide turned. The French War and the Revolutionary War put an end to the Great Awakening and were followed by the usual effects of warfare, the decay of piety and the growth of infidelity and profanity, immorality, intemperance, and vice. Americans became enamored of French skepticism. It became the fashion of scholarship to doubt the Bible, to scoff at the idea of the divinity of Christ, and to consider religion a superstition of the past, now outgrown by people of intelligence. The American colleges, originally established by the churches for the purpose of raising up and training Christian leaders for both church and state, naturally adopted the ideas of the scholars. They became hotbeds of infidelity; students paraded their unbelief by calling one another by the names of the French skeptics and infidels. It was said that in 1792 Princeton had only one student who made any profession of being a Christian. Yale was in much the same condition. Agnostics and infidels organized to overthrow Christianity. General Henry Dearborn said of the churches: "So long as these temples stand we cannot hope for good government." Indeed even in many of the larger towns there were no places of worship. George Washington said that he had more fear for the safety of the Republic in those godless days than he had in the darkest days of the Revolutionary War.

However, in the blackest hour light began to dawn. Simultaneously in the First Baptist Church in Boston and in North Yarmouth, Maine, a spiritual awakening began. For twelve glorious years the tide rose, each individual church feeling the influence of it in its own field. There were no vocational evangelists. The pastors were used of God in their own churches. Nor did the formerly atheistic colleges fail to share the influence of the spirit of God. Lyman Beecher said: "All infidelity skulked and hid its head." President Timothy Dwight of Yale was greatly used of God, and in 1802 a revival broke

22

out in Yale that promised to sweep the whole student body into the Kingdom of God. Wave followed wave of revival in Yale, and other American colleges were equally blessed. The tide had turned so completely that if Rip Van Winkle had gone to sleep in the period of infidelity he would never have recognized the reborn America in which he might have awakened some years later.

The country was entirely changed; sobriety and chastity had replaced drunkenness, dissoluteness, and immorality. The American Tract Society and the American Bible Society came into existence on the crest of this tidal wave. Men whose lives had been changed in the cleansing flood not only longed to see their neighbors transformed by the power of Christ, but their sympathies were also broadened and extended to enfold people whom they had never seen. Adoniram Judson and Luther Rice set out for foreign climes as Saul and Barnabas had done when the impulse for evangelism overflowed from Antioch to the whole known world; and whereas Judson and Rice had turned eastward, with the same missionary passion born of evangelism, John Mason Peck set his face toward the unevangelized Middle West in the first home missionary movement. Christian education was borne forward on the tide. The American Sunday School Union was organized, and theological seminaries were formed in order that the revived churches might be provided with intelligent and trained leadership. The intellectual impulse born of evangelism also found expression in religious journalism, a number of Christian and denominational papers and magazines being brought into existence at this time of spiritual awakening.

A graph of the ebb and flow of evangelism would resemble a chart of the dips and peaks of business in the United States. In fact it would be interesting to study the relation of times of depression and prosperity to the decline and increase in godliness among the people. The period preceding 1857 had been a time of greater prosperity than the United States had ever experienced. The discovery of gold in California had incited the people with the lust for riches; new settlements sprang up almost overnight, and gambling, drunkenness, and immorality again increased among those who forgot God in the rush for gold. There was also a mad competition in railroad building as steel rails eagerly reached out as rapidly as possible toward the gold fields and the new settlements. Gold had gotten into the blood of the people, and gambling and speculation rose to fever heat.

In 1857 the inevitable reaction set in. The panic of that year, with its many bank failures and the bankruptcy of great railroad companies, is so well known that it is unnecessary to describe it in these pages. In all parts of the country thousands of persons were thrown out of employment; despair settled upon the formerly exuberant population. As it so frequently happens when men come to the end of their own resources, they turned to God. Prayer meetings started in New York city spread to all parts of the country. A traveler making his way from Omaha to Boston said: "There is in America a prayer meeting two thousand miles long." The movement in the direction of prayer was spontaneous on the part of the people. It was not directed by evangelists or ministers. In fact under this great movement of the spirit laymen came into their own. To an extent, at least, the Reformation had rescued the church from the domination of the clergy and made it a church of the people, but at this particular time lay leadership became pronounced. There was little preaching in the revival of 1858. It was distinctively a revival of prayer. The prayer meetings had been inaugurated for the comfort of the people crushed in spirit by the financial panic, but "the wind bloweth where it listeth," and the meetings designed to bring comfort brought both comfort and salvation to the people who were converted in the prayer meetings and in their homes. Quite naturally those who prayed were conditioned by prayer to put forth effort to win their fellows for Christ. The results were remarkable. During a single year half a million converts were received into the churches. It is said that there were fifty thousand converted weekly. In Philadelphia alone ten thousand new converts were added to the churches of that city. Denominational lines were forgotten, and people of all creeds were brought together on the common ground of prayer.

Again today the tide is out. We have reached what seems to correspond to the lowest point in the cycle described at the beginning of this chapter. Not only is our world what Sorokin calls it "a sensate world," a world of the senses in which men live for sensual satisfactions, but because it is a sensate world it is a sick world, and a world as foolish as that woman in one of our hospitals who waved the doctor away one morning when he came to her bedside, saying petulantly: "I'm too sick to see you today, doctor, some other day." It is the sick that need a physician, and the sicker they are the more they need the physician. Or, our world is like the man who says: "I'm very sick today, but don't worry about me; in a day or so I'll be out and around again." There are no grounds today for such easy optimism. We cannot and must not close our eyes to the tragic picture of things as they are, like that bishop of the Church of England who, it is said, had a row of trees planted around his comfortable home to conceal the unpleasant sight of a near-by slaughterhouse. Although the trees hid the abattoir from view, they could not prevent the stench of it from reaching the fastidious nostrils of the bishop. We cannot escape our world. Instead of making such an attempt we must do what we can to cure it. Time is no longer with us. It may be now or never. The picture in the book of Revelation of an angel, with one foot on the sea and the other on the earth, declaring that "there should be time no longer," is becoming more real and present to us. Can there be yet another spiritual awakening in America?

"Evangelism is outmoded" men say. "This is the atomic age. Things that have been in the past cannot be today." But men have always said something of that sort. The word of John Wesley's father to the boy who was destined to lead the great evangelical awakening needs to be spoken again. Laying his hand upon his son's head, the old clergyman would say: "Be steady. The Christian faith will surely revive in this kingdom. You shall see it though I shall not."

On the top of the highest hill overlooking the railroad station at Fort Benton, Montana, there is a monument. Beside the monument there stands a statue of a collie. Beneath it white stones spell the name "Shep." Some years ago a sheepherder came to that little community bringing Shep with him. After a time the sheepherder became ill and was taken away on a train to a hospital. He never came back. From that time on Shep met every train that pulled into Fort Benton, awaiting his master's return. One day, in his eagerness, the faithful dog stepped into the path of a train and was killed. The people of the town were so moved by the faithfulness of the dog that they buried him on the hill and raised a fund to set up a monument to him. Despite the unbelief of men, let us dare to believe that our Master, the great shepherd of the sheep, will return in power to gather in both the "lost sheep of the house of Israel" and the "other sheep . . . which are not of this fold" in a sweeping spiritual awakening. Our Master is not dead. The Holy Spirit can yet "convict the world in respect of sin, and of righteousness, and of judgment."

No one will dispute the fact that the wind and the tide are contrary to us. But what is there in God's universe that is actually impossible? "Impossible?" asked Mirabeau. "Never name to me that blockhead of a word." If anyone had told us that fish could swim up a waterfall, we would have said that's impossible, but in the Columbia River some of us have seen both small and large salmon arrive at a wall of water pouring down over the rocks, hesitate for a moment or two before that seemingly impossible hurdle, flip their tails impatiently, and then, with what seems little effort, they swim straight up the wall of water. Presently they are in the comparatively smooth water above the falls. Every year at the spawning season these fish make their way up the Columbia River past many such apparently insurmountable barriers. It is the nature of the salmon to rise above such barriers, and it is the very nature of Christians to surmount impossible barriers, especially when they are driven by the impulse to see new-born souls brought into God's Kingdom.

Is it not true that the United States is more ready for a revival today than England was in John Wesley's day? Speaking of religion in England today, Cecil Northcott said: "The combustible material for a glorious conflagration is here." It is here in the United States as well. Monsignor Fulton J. Sheen says: "There are ten million Americans who are hungry for conversion today. The age of indifference to religion is ended." "Come from the four winds, O Spirit, and breathe upon the slain that they may live," that the church and the land may experience a resurrection.

A sweeping revival is usually preceded by a period of spiritual indifference and widespread hopelessness. Men grow impatient with the church and its innocuous desuetude, and desert its altars, believing that it is archaic and about to pass away. The church loses its sense of mission and occupies itself with a purposeless round of secondary pursuits. Its standards of life and conduct are debased until it seems that like the church at Laodicea, the Lord is ready to spew it out. Yet resurrection can come only after death, recovery only after illness, and

> At two o'clock in the morning, if you open your
> window and listen,
> You will hear the feet of the wind that is going
> to call the sun,
> And the trees in the shadow rustle and the trees
> in the moonlight glisten,
> And 'though it is deep, dark night, you feel
> the night is done.[1]

An awakening will not come automatically, however, as does the dawn or high tide in the ocean. It will not come of itself. Working with God we must help to bring the revival.

[1] From "The Dawn Wind," from *Rudyard Kipling's Verse Book*. Copyright 1891, 1934 by Rudyard Kipling. Reprinted by permission of Mrs. George Bambridge and Doubleday & Company, Inc.

In the Finger Lakes region of New York state one can see the points of three scythes protruding from the trunk of a huge Balm of Gilead tree. Long years ago the owner of the farmhouse near that tree hung his scythe in the crotch of the then small sapling and joined the Northern forces in the Civil War. He died of wounds in a Confederate hospital. Years later, when this country was plunged into World War I, two young men from this same farm also hung their scythes in the same tree and went overseas to help "make the world safe for democracy." The handles of the scythes have rotted away, but the growing tree has encased the blades in its now massive trunk until only a few inches of them remain visible.

Just beyond the farm is a town significantly named Waterloo. Generations of God's people have hung their scythes on the trees in an atmosphere unfriendly to evangelism, as once their spiritual ancestors hung their harps on the willows by the rivers of Babylon, refusing to sing the Lord's songs in a strange land. Again and again the fields have turned white unto harvest but the scythes of the saints remained hanging on the trees until the summer was over, the harvest was passed, men were not saved, and the church soon came to its Waterloo. Again there comes the call for reapers. May the Lord of the harvest thrust forth laborers into his harvest. May the new day of opportunity not pass and find us unprofitable sons—sleeping in harvest.

How can we bring back the flood tide? How can we rediscover, cleanse of its incrustation of much unfortunate tradition, and lift to its proper place at the top of the arch the lost capstone? A mother promised her two boys, eight and ten years of age, their first airplane trip. The boys were in a gleeful state of excitement when they arrived at the airport. A giant four motored plane was just taking off. They watched it rise and start on its flight. Presently the younger of the boys began to cry.

"Why, son, what is the matter?" his mother asked.

"I don't want to go up in an airplane!"

"Why not?"

"Look at that," he said as he pointed to the plane that had become a tiny speck in the sky. "I don't want to get little like that."

Some of us are afraid that if we get nearer to God we will become small and narrow like some of those people who pray the pharisaical prayer, "I thank thee that I am more spiritual than other men." But the tide usually returns when those who have risen highest in humble but true spirituality, and who are nearest God, realize how far from him they actually are and draw nearer to him. They do not grow smaller but greater in vision and capacity. Drawing nearer to God they lift the eyes of those who are still a little farther away and they are encouraged by the example of the people a little higher up. They begin to feel that nearness to God is not fanatical; it does not make one little or narrow if the people they admire are nearer God and are more vital and joyous than ever they were before. We get into grief not when we rise too high, but when we do not go high enough. From his porch in Salt Lake City a friend pointed out to me the peak on which an airplane had crashed. He said: "The marks on that peak showed that if the pilot had gone only six feet higher he would have cleared the peak and found the infinite stretches of space out beyond it." Our troubles are usually caused by our remaining on too low a level. When people who before were neither hot nor cold are drawn closer to God, they develop a new love for him and for his house, together with a new desire to see men won for Christ. The process continues until the church develops what should always be its normal concern for a lost world. In his lectures on evangelism Charles G. Finney says an awakening comes when the wickedness of the wicked grieves and distresses God's people.

It may seem trite to say that spiritual awakening comes only through the vicarious suffering of God's people over sin and their strong crying to God, but if it is trite it is also true. There is an enormous price to be paid. A doorway was to be cut through the solid masonry of a very old church building. The walls were almost three feet thick. One wondered how in the old days men ever lifted such enormous blocks of stone to such heights, as one wonders how workmen lifted to their places the great blocks in the pyramids. That is also our modern problem—how to lift the capstone of the arch to its proper place. It can be done only at enormous cost by men who are willing to give their blood, if need be, that the wonder may be wrought in a world where all the forces of modernity seem unalterably set against the successful consummation of such effort. It can be done only by men who will a spiritual awakening as the Apostle Paul willed the salvation of the Roman Empire, and as John Knox willed the salvation of his beloved Scotland. Nothing can stand before such indomitable will, especially as it runs parallel to the will of God. Men usually find it possible to accomplish that which they really want to accomplish. We can see a spiritual awakening in our day if we want it deeply, desperately as blind men long for light; as starving men yearn for food; as men wanted rain in the days of Jeremiah, when the heavens were shut up for three years; as lean, lonely men longed for liberty while they were confined in prison camps on Bataan and in Japan. Wanting it, praying for it, working for it, we shall not be denied.

III

Lifting the Stone

THE CONGREGATION OF A CHURCH in the eastern part of the United States was thrown into consternation by the announcement of city officials that the street alongside the church was to be widened. This meant that the near side of the street would cut through the center of their noble building. What to do? Contractors said it would be impossible to move so large a brick building, but at length one contractor said: "Show us the money, and we'll move the building." Land on the opposite side was acquired and a new foundation was built upon it. The contractor put fifty jackscrews under the church and engaged two hundred workmen. He put four men at each of the jackscrews. When all was in readiness a signal was given, and all the men began to move together turning the jackscrews. Gradually, and without noticeable movement, the great building began to rise. In time it was moved to its new location.

We are all conscious that probably few of our churches are where they should be today. Each must be lifted and moved to the place God would have it occupy in the life of the community. To move it is a task demanding more than human power, but if God's people will all move together at the jackscrews of prayer the invisible power will eventually become apparent in the visible rising of the church and its moving into a commanding position in the life of the community.

Canon Hay Aitken once said:

The surest sign of the approach of a season of revival is the disposition to pray for it, which, while it is itself the product of the divine influence, may be regarded as the human response to God's call, which is the condition of the further extension of that spiritual influence.

Someone recently called my attention to the fact that the Greek word *deomai*, which is the basic word for the act of praying, means first of all to be in want of, to feel the need of, to be utterly devoid of.

In his book *Revivals, Their Laws and Leaders* James Burns tells about the disposition to prayer out of the crushing sense of need and inadequacy that precedes revival. He says:

> God's people react in revulsion to the wickedness and corruption of the world about them. Unable to cope with a civilization moving in the direction of moral chaos, in their helplessness men cry out to God for help. Prayer eventually becomes insistent, importunate, irresistible. Not only do faithful men pray in secret; they gather kindred spirits. The soul anguish is communicated from one to the other and thus intensified.

Describing the period preceding the great evangelical awakening in England, Burns says:

> Slowly the national conscience, so long dormant, began to wake up. Men began to sicken at the prevailing ungodliness; a sense of nausea and unrest began to show itself, along with a craving for better things. In the night of sin, amid its passions and debaucheries, men had forgotten God; but when the night was past, and the raw morning began to break, they awoke to a sense of their misery, to a shame of their evil courses, to a shuddering consciousness of how far they had been led astray, and to a bitter self-loathing and disgust. Yet more was needed. To bring fresh hope and joy to an age worn out and surfeited with sin, a revival was needed. Men longed for a breath of God to blow upon the land, to sweep away its miasmas and heavy poisoned atmosphere, and bring back to it the joyous sunshine of God's presence and the gladness and freshness of a living faith. Once more human nature was declaring that the way of transgressors is hard, that sin has no final empire over the human heart, that for the soul of man there is no rest except in God. Gradually the longing for better things grew in the hearts of the best men and women of the age, and the cry once more went up to God full of passionate entreaty, the cry for forgiveness, for renewal, for a fresh awakening to the blessedness of the spiritual life. The cry was heard. The hour and the man were

come. Into the life of England of that century, to dominate it and inspire it, there enters the prim, alert figure of John Wesley, Anglican, Methodist, Revivalist, and Man of God.[1]

Hurrying to an engagement through the crowded streets of Chicago recently, I passed one of those ubiquitous purveyors of a certain religious magazine, who usually stand mute and unnoticed at the side of the stream of humanity as it rushes past. Not so this colored man. He was repeating: "If you don't go to heaven while you're alive how do you expect to go to heaven when you die?" If an awakening is to come to America we must look to heaven for power.

A spiritual awakening is never the result of clever planning unless the machinery is empowered by heavenly potency. Machinery is necessary. It has its place. Ezekiel saw wheels within wheels, but he saw also that when the living creatures were lifted up the wheels were lifted up, and when the living creatures moved the wheels moved, for there is spirit in the wheels, and when the spirit is absent the wheels may revolve, but it is altogether without lasting result. Karl Heim puts it thus: "The machinery has come to a stop in a great factory run by electricity. The transmission system and all the machinery of the factory are closely examined by workmen. They finally discover the difficulty: the fuses in the basement have been blown out." It is futile to tinker with the machinery until we have connected with power from on high. "The fuses in the basement" explain the mystery of spiritual power.

> Away in foreign lands they wondered "how"
>   Their simple words had power!
> At home, the Christians, "two or three" had met
>   To pray an hour.
>
> Yes, we are always wondering, wondering "how"
>   Because we do not see
> Some one, unknown perhaps, and far away,
>   On bended knee.[2]

[1] By permission of James Clarke & Co., Ltd.
[2] Author unknown.

33

A blind white horse went round and round in circles for years, never knowing why, except that he was obeying the command of his master. He did not know that he was lifting great stones to their places in a growing cathedral, nor did he ever see the completed building; but he had an important part in the work. Although an awakening is so desperately needed, and although many signs point to its coming, no man knows when it may come. Nonetheless, in faithful obedience to the word of our Master that "men ought always to pray, and not to faint," let us continue at the essential work of intercession with confidence in the far-off interest of prayer.

Dwight L. Moody once preached in a North London church. The morning service was characterized by nothing unusual. At the close of the evening service, however, practically the whole congregation went into the inquiry room. The next day Moody went to Dublin, but an urgent message from the pastor of the North London church brought him back. He preached there for ten days, and four hundred persons were added to the membership of that church as a result. That did not happen by chance, nor was it wholly the effect of Moody's preaching. A shut-in member of that church had read an account of Moody's work in America. She prayed that he might visit her church. When her sister returned from worship the morning Moody preached and told her about the service, she said: "I know what that means: God has heard my prayers." Beyond all question he had. Moody believed that the prayers of this invalid woman, and the revival that resulted from them, was responsible for his return to England again the next year.

Prayerful parishioners can help produce powerful preaching. When a visitor had been shown to a seat in Charles Haddon Spurgeon's Metropolitan Tabernacle in London he became conscious of a murmur of voices around him. It did not surprise him because he was used to hearing the chatter of a gathering congregation, but as he settled down in the pew it became apparent to him that it was not conversation but those people were praying. They were saying: "God, bless Mr. Spurgeon today and give him a message that will reach the hearts of men." In such an atmosphere it would be almost impossible to imagine that souls would not be saved.

When J. Wilbur Chapman was invited to become pastor of Bethany Presbyterian Church in Philadelphia he was overwhelmed with a sense of inadequacy for the demands of that parish. He visited Spurgeon's tabernacle. At the close of a day, when God's presence had been especially marked in the services, Chapman expressed his gratitude to Spurgeon. Spurgeon replied: "Tut, tut, my brother, the blessing is from above. Every day and night thousands of people in London, and scores of thousands everywhere in the English-speaking world, are praying for the tabernacle and for me as the pastor. If you wish to have a soul-winning church get your people to pray." The world knows that Chapman followed Spurgeon's advice and his church experienced an almost constant revival.

Horatius Bonar said: "If the preaching of the gospel is to exercise a great power over mankind, it must be either by enlisting extraordinary men or by the endowing of ordinary men with extraordinary power." The people of almost any church can pray their minister into extraordinary power, and they cannot excuse themselves by insisting they have no time to pray. Martin Luther used to say, "Prayer and provender hinder no man in his journey," and Thomas Hooker averred, "My chiefest employment is prayer. It is by means of it that I get everything else done."

A daily tryst with God does not have to wait upon ideal conditions. Rushing through the bowels of the earth in the subway, plowing the fields, washing dishes in the kitchen, or making beds in the bedroom, one may lift his heart to God and engage in the mightiest business in the world. The humble man nailing covers on boxes in the shipping room may be a partner with the Eternal in prayer. We are never so busy that we cannot pray. Let the Christian mothers pray. Someone has said that revival is largely the history of praying mothers. Years ago the superintendent of an inebriate asylum in Binghamton, New York, said: "Some men are sent here under compulsion —almost driven here by their friends; and no such men are ever cured. No man has ever gone from this asylum cured of inebriacy unless there was someone, a sister, a mother, a wife, a maiden, who prayed for him, hoped for him, and wept for him at home."

One of the chief points of weakness in the modern church is the prayer meeting, or in many instances the unblushing omission of this service, so essential to spiritual success. Many churches continue for years without a midweek service, and many others hold services almost wholly devoid of power. Officials of the church do not attend, and often when they do they are unwilling to lead in prayer. How often do we have earnest prayers for the salvation of lost men? Let us put forth determined effort to revive the midweek service and make it a real prayer meeting. As just another meeting in the course of the week, another preaching service, it may seem a fifth wheel in the organization, another claimant on an already overtaxed agenda, but as an "Hour of Power," aimed directly toward curing our national ills and lifting the capstone of evangelism to its place, it may again prove to be the powerhouse of the church.

William McCulloch was not an extraordinary man nor a "popular" preacher, but realizing the appalling needs of his people at Cambuslang, Scotland, he rose at five each morning to pray and study the Bible. He encouraged his people to unite in praying bands that they might lift the church into newness of spiritual life. Out of that fellowship of prayer came the demand for a midweek service. When it had been arranged for the service to be held each Thursday evening, the prayers of pastor and people became still more earnest and importunate. Monday, Tuesday, and Wednesday the people gathered at the manse for intercession. The blessing of the Almighty came down on the Thursday night meeting. McCulloch spoke slowly and cautiously, as he always did, but when he had finished it was evident that the church had been lifted into new power and life. Fifty people followed the minister to his manse where the whole night was spent in instructing the converts in the way of Christ. The following day the church was opened, and night after night for twelve weeks McCulloch preached to people under deep conviction, many of whom were won for Christ.

The revival in Cambuslang encouraged the Scots of Kilsyth to pray for revival. They prayed for years without seeing any result. Then one day when William Chalmers Burns preached in his Kilsyth pulpit on the text "Thy people shall be willing in the day of thy power," he related how long before, John Livingston, a native of their own community, in preparation for a communion service, spent a whole night in prayer. God gave Livingston such a vision of his holiness and glory that the young preacher was overcome with a sense of his own unworthiness and he fled into the fields to escape the responsibility of standing as God's representative before the people. It was only when his friends found him and prevailed upon him to return that he came into the pulpit. Then he was suddenly clothed with power from on high. Five hundred persons were converted through the single sermon preached that day.

Many years later, as Burns related the story, the people were moved again as they had been on that day when John Livingston preached. Like the Cambuslang church, the Kilsyth church was then opened for services every night, and during many months, night after night, men declared themselves for Christ. Kilsyth had been a drunken community.

All bargains and payments had been made over "the friendly glass." The session clerk had his office in the public house, where he speedily became a victim of the prevailing sin, while the typical funeral service was composed of long prayers interspersed with rounds of drinking. Now drink received a fatal blow. The town was cleansed from its vice. Loom shops became places of prayer, and many a home became a Bethel.

When Robert McCheyne first came to Dundee "he was appalled by its heathenism." He mourned its "idolatry and hardness of heart," and the feeble influence of the surviving church. But with the fortitude of faith he set himself to his task. Very soon he established a weekly prayer meeting on Thursday evening, and there he read to his people or told them the story of God's marvelous work in past revivals. Once again, as so often before and since, the seed of the great harvest was sown in the prayer meeting. McCheyne gave himself constantly to counseling with the people who sought him out. The prayer meeting grew, but McCheyne's health broke, and while he was absent from his pulpit, William C. Burns took his place. He told the people of Dundee about the gracious revival at Kilsyth, and invited those who felt the need of an outpouring of the spirit to convert men to remain after service. About a hundred stayed. The whole group was bathed in tears. That night the great work began, and for four months the church was open and crowded every night. The whole city of Dundee was moved. For a time no less than thirty-nine prayer meetings were held weekly in connection with this church, and whole multitudes of men and women were gloriously converted.

It may be well at times to divide the church prayer meeting into small prayer groups for part of the service, various groups going into different rooms where they may kneel in small circles of prayer. Many persons who are reluctant to lead in audible prayer in a larger gathering will participate in informal prayer in a small group, and their prayers will be more genuine and less self-conscious.

In a church where the midweek service was attended by no more than a dozen persons, and the gatherings were lifeless, the pastor tried the experiment of dividing the few attendants into small congenial groups, young people praying together in one group, women in another, the deacons in another. Definite objects of prayer were set before the groups. There resulted such revival in the hearts of the people that they began to share with others their revitalized spiritual experience. Soon these others came seeking for themselves what their friends had received, and within an incredibly short time instead of a dozen there were fifty in attendance, some of them being unchurched persons who, in the fellowship of Christ's people, found the Saviour and were soon received into the membership of the church. The small groups, moving together at the jackscrews of prayer, lifted the whole church into newness of life.

In addition to the midweek prayer service of the church, little groups of earnest people should gather together regularly for prayer. During World War II the pastor of a Mexican church, realizing that there were mothers in his membership who were anxious for their soldier sons at the front, invited any who were interested to meet him at the church on a certain week night evening to pray for their lads. He suggested that they bring the most recent letters from their boys in order that the prayers might be more specifically directed to their needs. Instead of the two or three mothers he had expected twenty women came to the meeting. The result of that first gathering was such that those who attended urged the pastor to arrange other meetings. They also told their friends about their experience and many of these friends, Catholics as well as Protestants, began to attend. Several of them asked to be received into the church on profession of their faith.

When Monsignor Fulton J. Sheen, nationally-known radio speaker, was an assistant pastor, "back of the yards," according to the *Reader's Digest*, a girl who proclaimed herself the "worst girl in town," just out of the state reformatory for girls, stopped at the church door. She did it only to please her mother, she said. She herself had made a contract with the devil.

"Stay here and pray," pleaded the priest, but she turned away. "You'll come back," the priest said. "You'll come back tonight."

The only way the young man could fight the devil was through prayer. He asked everyone who came into the church that day to pray an hour for the girl. After everyone else had gone he himself knelt in prayer for her. "It was long after midnight when he heard the click-clack of heels coming down the marble aisle." Then he knew she was kneeling beside him. He heard her weeping. That lost soul is "a wonderful woman today."

Two university professors agreed to visit another professor of the same university to invite him to identify himself with

Christ and the church, but when they arrived in front of his home they asked themselves why they had agreed to expose themselves to what he would probably say during the interview. The head of the economics department of the school, he was known often to speak slurringly of the church and sometimes of religion itself. The two professors did not go up the steps of the porch at once. Instead they walked around the block. Finally they went in to talk with their colleague, and to their surprise they found that the people praying at the church had already reached him through the throne of grace, and within twenty minutes they had led him to a decision for Christ.

If we would lift the church of our day and our community, and bring upon it times of refreshing, let us repair to the jackscrews of prayer. When the low ebb of the spiritual tide in the new field in which a minister recently settled became evident to him, he said to his people: "Only God can save this church. We must look to him every day. I will be in the church for prayer at 9 A.M. daily. You who believe in the God who forgives and answers prayer, join me wherever you are. Drop into the church and pray with me if ever you can." Seldom more than two or three joined him. Sometimes he prayed alone. Nonetheless the very fact that the minister and some of the people were praying regularly roused the hope and expectation of the church. Before long regular attendance at the church services increased, church officers confessed their sins and asked God's forgiveness, people were converted, the church was refreshed and the community was moved. It was so in the American Awakening in 1858. By the very evil of the times, the church was driven to its knees. Then a wonderful thing happened.

In answer to the church's united cry, ascending from all parts of the land, the Spirit of God, in a very quiet way, and suddenly, throughout the whole extent of the United States, renewed the church's life, and awakened in the community around it a great thirst for God. Thus it came about that, in the same city, the movement began at the same time in different quarters and proceeded for a while before the fact became generally known. As in the miracle of II Kings 3, into the thirsty valley, filled with ditches by the labour of believing, praying men, there came on a sudden the quiet flow of the gracious Spirit, and in a moment the churches became channels brimming with the living water.

In Jayne's Hall 4,000 met daily to wait upon God. Drawn from every class, they were massed together in a great stillness, broken only for a while by the sobs of the penitent. Then brief, earnest prayers would be offered, often only a few broken sentences. The presence of God, vividly realized, produced a marvelous quietude and orderliness. Brief exhortations, the repetition of a single text, pierced the heart like a knife. At the end of the hour the multitude quietly dispersed and returned to business, but they looked as Jacob looked when the sun rose upon Penuel.[3]

It was said that as they drew near American ports, ships seemed to come "within a definite zone of heavenly influence. Ship after ship arrived with the same tale of sudden conviction and conversion. It was wonderful beyond words! In one ship a captain and the entire crew of thirty men found Christ out at sea and entered the harbor rejoicing." Perhaps the most striking awakening took place on a battleship. The U. S. S. *North Carolina* was in New York harbor. Four men decided to meet for prayer. They were so filled with joy that they burst into song.

The strange sweet strain rose to the decks above, and there created a great astonishment. Their ungodly shipmates came running down. They came to mock, but the mighty power of God had been liberated by rejoicing faith. It gripped them, and in one moment their derisive laugh was changed into the cry of penitent sinners! Great fellows, giants in stature, and many of them giants in sin, were literally smitten down, and knelt humbly beside the four like little children. A most gracious work straightway began in the depths of the great ship.[4]

Home prayer meetings have lifted many a church into newness of life. One church held eleven such meetings each night

[3] *Old-Time Revivals*. By John Shearer. By permission of the author.
[4] *Ibid*.

41

for a week in the homes of members. The people were so stirred by them that the church planned similar meetings at stated periods during the year. Such prayer meetings proved so dynamic in another church that at the close of the week eight persons presented themselves for church membership, and the deacons and deaconesses were so moved by the meetings that, without being asked, they volunteered to call upon all the members of the church during the next week.

Whether singly, in the midweek services, or in small groups, when God's people pray they shall "be aware of answer coming down."

" 'Till the dim earth is luminous with the light of the white dawn, from some far-hidden shore."

IV

A Stone of Stumbling

WHEN THE DINING CAR WAITER handed him the menu a traveler was intrigued by the exciting picture on the cover, representing three men pouring yellow molten steel from a huge crucible that glowed blood-red in the reflection of the liquid metal. In imagination he could see that steel being hammered out into miles on miles of rails girding the prairies, the "purple mountain majesties," and "the fruited plains" in the United States. The traveler continued to study the compelling picture of action, suggesting energy poured across a continent, providing vitality for a nation's life, trade, and commerce, and the crimson priests of commerce pouring out molten steel seemed changed into the great High Priest of our profession, with a basin pouring blood at the base of the altar of the tabernacle. That is a still more exciting picture, for blood is life and energy. It will not become hardened steel, but it will go throbbing and pulsating into the personalities of redeemed men, and moving out through them in redemptive service.

Blood stands for the cleansing of redemption, the washing of regeneration. As the high priest of the Old Testament cleansed another tabernacle built by men's hands, with the blood of sacrificial bulls and goats, so our High Priest cleanses the "true tabernacle, which the Lord pitched, and not man," the inner sanctuary of the soul of man, not with the blood of bulls and goats but with his own blood poured out on Calvary. Blood stands for propitiation and cleansing, but it stands also for the transmissive element in redemption.

When a group of young people heard of the efforts of their denomination to restore the mission properties destroyed in World War II, they determined to have a part in the effort. They had little money, but they had the abundant life of

43

youth; and they went to the blood bank at their local hospital and gave their blood, thus raising two thousand dollars for the fund. They said: "Christ gave his blood for us. Why should we not give our blood for him?" They had envisaged a basic idea of the Christian life. Those who receive life from Christ are trustees of the divine deposit, responsible to pass it on to others. Evangelism is an exceedingly costly thing. It takes blood. A spiritual awakening is not the easy bloodless experience many good people conceive it to be. The people of God must be prepared to pay the full price.

In the days of Amos the people were looking forward to the day of the Lord, but the prophet told them of the enormous cost and the pain of that day. In revival, judgment begins at the house of the Lord. When the church has been realistic about a spiritual awakening, it has been reluctant to pay the price, and the revival has often come outside of the organized church, as when a man has nailed his theses on the door of a cathedral, or a man, driven from the church, has stood upon his father's tombstone to preach, or the revival has come, as Professor Kenneth Latourette tells us in his history of the church, out of the younger churches rather than out of the places where Christianity is more deeply entrenched. For a revival causes the church humiliation, the frank admission of sin and failure to do its duty, of godless living, and blighting worldliness. It calls the church to reconsecration, to the forsaking of the ways of ease and luxury, to bloodletting. It is blood that supplies energy. When the blood is low we seem listless, dull, apathetic. When the church is anemic there are long periods of spiritual deadness. Christian people live like the worldlings about them, for wealth and personal gratification. They are not willing to take the way of the cross. It is only when the cross becomes vivid through evangelism, and Christlike love invades their hearts, that they forget self.

We would like a painless Christianity, but a painless Christianity is no Christianity at all. All true Christianity is related to the cross. Many of us claim to be Christians when we are more like Buddhists. What a delightfully easy religion is

Buddhism! Not a painful religion but a religion that frees you from all concern and desire. See that man on a cross, arms extended, hands nailed, forehead bloody, frame gaunt from fasting and nights spent in prayer, side gashed—blood flowing from it—ghastly sight! But look yonder at Buddha, eyes closed in repose, hands gently folded, great pouch of a well-fed belly, layer on layer of fat, face wreathed in a smile of contentment and aloofness. How simple it would be to turn from the cross with its blood and seat ourselves by the side of Buddha. How much more comfortable to follow the course pursued by Erasmus, the gentle humanist of Holland, who agreed with the principles of Martin Luther and advocated Catholic reforms but who, when Luther's followers challenged him to ally himself publicly with their leader, asked: "Why should I lose my living or my head?" He recognized the abominations of the Roman Church. He asserted that instead of saying their prayers the monks were eating gingerbread that they might the more enjoy their beer, but he never actually broke with the church and he left Luther to fight alone. If at the Diet of Worms he had stood with Luther he might have proved an almost indispensable ally, yet like the rich young ruler, who turned away when he learned the cost of discipleship, and the multitudes that followed Jesus until he began to talk about the cross and bloodletting, he took the easier way. Savonarola, on the other hand, tortured and degraded, dying on the gallows, rose at that time to greater heights than ever he did in preaching from the pulpit of St. Mark's.

When the comfortable, self-seeking Festus observed the abandon with which Paul served his Lord, he said what the worldling says of all self-abnegating Christians: "Paul, thou art mad"; but as Ian Maclaren remarks: "Why should a gladiator be sane and St. Paul be mad? If any man believes that the Kingdom of God will remain when this world has disappeared like a shadow, then he has a right to fling away all that he possesses, and himself too for its advancement and victory."

In times of spiritual awakening men recapture the sacrificial spirit that characterized their Lord, the Apostle Paul, and other

45

God-intoxicated immortals who counted not their lives dear unto themselves.

My subject in speaking at the meeting of a group of churches was "The Atoning Christ in an Atomic Age." Can Christ capture the atomic age as once he captured the Roman Empire? Only an atoning Christ can do it.

Whether or not Constantine actually saw in the sky the words "In hoc signo vinces," it is everlastingly true that Christian victory comes only through the cross. Though the cross has always been a stone of stumbling, "unto the Jews a stumbling block, and unto the Greeks foolishness," yet it is by the blood of the Lamb shed on the cross that Satan is overcome. It is said that after conquering almost the whole of Europe, Napoleon spread out a map of that continent and, putting his finger on the British Isles, said: "Were it not for that red spot I would conquer the world." So we may say: "Were it not for that red spot called Calvary, sin and Satan would soon conquer all." No denomination, or group within any denomination, that belittles or rejects the cross knows anything of the power of evangelism. They never move great companies of men; they know nothing of the healthy enthusiasm of evangelicalism. On the other hand, each major revival in history has emphasized some distinctive doctrine, but every one of them has had one message in common—the message of the cross, of redeeming love, of a Saviour who died that we might live. Nor in great revivals is the cross preached merely as a way of escape. It is at once the way of the Redeemer and the way of the redeemed. The atonement of our Lord was a blood atonement. Paul says: "I may almost say, all things are cleansed with blood, and apart from shedding of blood there is no remission." That is an inescapable and all-pervading principle of the Kingdom. We have entered into a new and frightening period of the world's history. It may be conquered only as John tells us the saints overcame Satan, "by the blood of the Lamb" that can cleanse the life of the individual, the church, the nation, and the world, and supply the spiritual energy by which the new

46

forces now in the hands of modern man may be guided toward his good rather than toward the annihilation of all humanity.

What do we mean by the blood of Christ? Not a material substance surely. None of us have actually been immersed in the material blood of Christ that left his body when he died on the cross and that was soaked up by the sacred soil of Calvary. To believe that we could be redeemed by a material substance would mean a mechanical and material salvation more like paganism, the rabbis' ideas of Judaism, or Roman Catholicism, than the spiritual salvation presented in the New Testament. Let the Bible explain itself. In the Old Testament we are told that when a hunter killed an animal he was to let all the blood out of the body, "for the blood is the life." When we look into the communion cup we contemplate the blood of Christ which was his life, his personality. We see his purity, his holiness, his obedience to his Father, his love, his self-giving. Then we realize that he died upon the cross and shed his blood that we might become "partakers of the divine life." When Christ enters within us spiritually through our faith he pours his life, his love, his personality, and his vital energy into us. Of course no one will consider this facet of the vast transaction of the cross a total explanation of that mystery which has baffled the greatest theological minds of all ages. Nonetheless the explanation attempts to point a basic principle of the Kingdom of God: that deliverance from sin is never without pain, never without the pouring out of life and personality into another's life.

Men are redeemed as we make known to them this mystery hidden for long ages but now made plain, that Christ may enter within us and live in us, the hope of glory. Satan is overcome by the blood of the Lamb and the word of the Christian's testimony. Witnessing is not easy. A layman said to his pastor: "I will give you one thousand dollars if you will let me off from the visitation evangelistic campaign." During the Civil War men could hire substitutes to take their places, but in this warfare there are no substitutes. There can be no substitute witnesses, for a witness is one who has seen something personally

and who testifies to what he has seen. A man who has experienced Christ is in duty bound to testify to what he has experienced. No one can witness but those who know Christ, and
that witness must be given not only in the friendly atmosphere of the church but in the unfriendly atmosphere of the
world, sometimes in the face of intense opposition and persecution. In the verse mentioned above, Christian testimony is
set between two pools of blood—the blood of the Lamb on
one side and the blood of the redeemed on the other. This is
the only way of redemption—pouring out one's life and love
and personality into another. Salvation comes to lost men in
no other way. It requires suffering. Blood stands for sacrifice,
suffering, self-giving. Black men, held in slavery in the United
States, were set free only when men suffered, shed their blood,
and died. If Satan and sin are to be overcome it will be by blood,
the blood of the Lamb of God and the word of the blood-
bought testifying to his blood. Someone must speak for God,
not only in a cushioned pulpit but in homes, stores, factories,
and on the street. God could not look benignly down on- a
lost world and say, "Be thou saved."

It is by no breath,
Turn of eye, wave of hand, that Salvation joins issue with death.[1]

In the famous Negro play *Green Pastures* men plead with
"the Lawd" to come down and save them, but he replies, "I
ain't a-comin' down." But he did come down and on an old
rugged cross he identified himself with sinful humanity and
shed his blood that they might be saved. When Jean Valjean
would save Marius he had to go down into the sewers of Paris,
and when an angel would release Peter from prison the angel
had to go into the prison. The saving of men has always cost
terribly. When God created the world he spake and it was
done; when he created man he breathed into him and he became a living soul; but when God would save man he had to
bleed for him. Salvation cost the Son of God his life and it
will cost us our lives.

[1] Robert Browning.

48

In the twelfth chapter of Romans, Paul says: "I beseech you therefore, brethren, . . . that ye present your bodies a living sacrifice, holy, acceptable unto God." To what does the word "therefore" refer? To the marvelous revelation of this great book that God has, by the death of his Son, provided salvation by faith. This is the mercy of God; he was done to death for us. His blood poured out. Therefore by the mercy of God we appeal that you match his sacrifice, which was unto death with a living sacrifice, that your blood still in your veins—your life energy—may be a living daily sacrifice to God and his Kingdom, not the letting of material blood but the spiritual self-giving of your very body to his service. Paul himself asked that he might know the fellowship of Christ's sufferings, and he said: "I fill up in my body that which is behind of the sufferings of Christ." Just what that means we may not fully comprehend, but we know it indicates that as the personality of Christ was sacrificially poured into us, that same spiritual energy must by us be poured into others.

J. H. Jowett once said, "When we cease to bleed we cease to bless." As birth comes through travail, so the new birth comes through spiritual travail, which Paul had in mind when he said: "My little children, of whom I travail in birth again until Christ be formed in you." And so he followed in his footsteps of whom it was prophesied: "He shall see of the travail of his soul, and shall be satisfied." It is the vicarious spirit of David, when in his poem "Saul," Browning makes him say:

See the King—I would help him but cannot, the wishes fall through.
Could I wrestle to raise him from sorrow, grow poor to enrich,
To fill up his life, starve my own out, I would—knowing which,
I know that my service is perfect. Oh, speak through me now!

God does speak through the valiant vicarious who have that deep spiritual concern for others, the spirit of Moses, who asked: "Wilt thou forgive their sin—; and if not, blot me, I pray thee, out of thy book which thou hast written," and Paul, who said: "I could wish that myself were accursed from Christ for my brethren, my kinsmen according to the flesh." Such vicarious suffering comes close to atonement. It will not be denied. It is the spirit that wins men and continents to the atoning Christ. If we are to be mighty hunters before the Lord we must say farewell to comfort and a soft life. A hunter will sit all day in a puddle of ice water in order to get a shot at a few ducks, tramp miles through cornfields, weary, almost exhausted, to get a few pheasants, or wear himself out to shoot a deer.

This is an age of illustration. Among the many pictures that came out of the explosion in Texas City in the spring of 1947 one of the most eloquent was a picture of a man asleep against a lamppost; utterly exhausted from long hours of rescue work, he had evidently slumped down and allowed himself the proverbial "forty winks" before going back to rescue other victims of the explosion. There was an emergency. Everyone was made conscious of it, and everyone was working day and night to help meet it. In the emergency of our age how many are working to the point of complete exhaustion to "rescue the perishing"? Yet the explosion of a single city in Texas, tragic as it was, is but a child's firecracker compared to the threatened explosion of a world. God's people must be prepared to say:

> Lead on, O King Eternal,
> . . . .
> Henceforth in fields of conquest
> Thy tents shall be our home.

The *Sunday School Times* once related the story of a sweet girl who was converted. At a testimony meeting some years later, in which others told of God's power in saving them from lives of gambling and other sinful pleasures, she arose and said: "Christ brought me a bigger salvation than any of you. He saved me from an easy armchair." How many of God's people are saved to that extent?

We cannot save men while we sit amid the comforts of our ivory towers. We must go to them "where the many toil and

50

suffer." The transfusion of spiritual life is no cold logical process of argumentation. It is the direct communication of life
from living soul to living soul, from the veins of one abounding in spiritual vitality to an anemic soul. In other forms of
Christian service we may give a cup of cold water, a crust, or a
check, but evangelism takes blood. If we are to experience a
spiritual awakening we must be prepared to pay the price in
blood and sweat and tears. We must show the courage of a
Luther, who, when he went to the Diet of Worms, was
touched by the gauntlet of a baron who said: "Pluck up thy
spirit, little monk. I have seen hard battles in my day but nor I
nor any knight in this company ever needed a stout heart more
than thou needest it now. If thou hast faith in these doctrines
of thine, little monk, go on." And Luther said: "Here I stand,
I can do no other, God help me." We must put Christ before
anything or anyone.

We must have the self-forgetfulness of George Whitefield,
who prayed: "When thou seest me in danger of nestling down,
put a thorn, in tender pity, into my nest." And again: "I am
determined to go on until I drop, to die fighting even though
it be on my stumps." On Whitefield's tomb at Newburyport
are the words: "As a soldier of the cross, humble, devout, ar-
dent, he put on the whole armor of God, preferring the honor
of Christ to his own interest, repose, reputation, or life."

V

Stand Upon the Rock

A MINISTER ANNOUNCED TO HIS PEOPLE: "A revival was to start in this church last week but it couldn't begin because the evangelist was tied up in another meeting. We expected the revival to begin today, but I just had a telegram from the evangelist that they are going on with the meeting in the other town, and I just want to say that if he doesn't come next week, we'll call it off and there will be no revival in this church."

In the last hundred years the churches have placed large dependence upon revivalistic evangelism under the leadership of vocational evangelists. Although a comparatively recent innovation, this method has borne much fruit. It has attracted community-wide, sometimes even nation-wide, attention to Christianity. It has produced a large hearing for the gospel. Held frequently on "neutral ground," in a tabernacle, tent, or public auditorium, it has attracted many outsiders who would be reluctant to enter a church building. It has thus developed a psychological vortex, making the gospel the object of popular attention and the subject of common conversation. The very dash and insistency of great mass evangelistic campaigns have led to decision many persons who needed this pressure to precipitate them into such a decisive step. Many a "hardened sinner" has come to decision under the stress of mass evangelism. Even after these many years in almost any large city one may meet persons who were converted in "Billy" Sunday's meetings after having been saloonkeepers, bartenders, drunkards, gamblers, or some other type of scandalous sinner.

Mass evangelism provides religion the emotional force which is so frequently lacking in ordinary church services, a force sufficient to shake Christians out of their complacency and rouse them to work for the salvation of lost men and women.

52

It often leads to the repentance and rededication of church members who have drifted into unchristian living. It is said that toward the latter part of his ministry Dwight L. Moody directed his messages to church members almost exclusively and Gipsy Smith did the same. I once asked him why. Gipsy replied: "Because the world knows the present condition of the church, and it listens to the preacher who is frank and honest about it. He wins the outsider by preaching to the church." However, the present generation, speaking generally, has turned away from mass evangelism. Many more people are being reached through other methods today than through this particular one. There were many abuses and many weaknesses connected with mass evangelism, yet no one can say that it will never again be revived and used effectively.

A series of meetings in which God's people concentrate upon things spiritual, giving up all other engagements to attend, listen, and work for the winning of men for Christ, however, is not dependent upon the coming of a vocational evangelist. Whether or not we may see definite results in first decisions for Christ as a result of a series of evangelistic meetings, such a series should be held in every church at least once a year for the spiritual benefit of the members. Some years ago the Presbyterian Church in the U. S. A. defined the purpose of a revival as "awakening of the church to an appreciation of its normal life in Christ and its opportunity to save souls." When the church is truly revived it saves souls. The Northern Baptist Convention said of the revival meeting:

God becomes distant and unreal to people because they become engrossed in the work and play of life. Let them agree together to push other things aside for a week or two or three and give every evening to opening their minds to God's truth with the prayer that God may make himself real to them again and take control of their lives anew, and they will not be disappointed.

Lin D. Cartwright says in his book *Evangelism for Today*:

The older members need constant remotivation. Herein is the chief value of the "revival" meeting. In preaching the gospel in

53

order to win new converts, the members of the church are led to espouse the cause with new enthusiasm and conviction. That is one of the reasons why an evangelistic spirit tends through the years to develop a congregation of loyal devotion and of high spiritual quality.[1]

The regular services of the church should be evangelistic. Men should be won for Christ week after week by the regular preaching of the pastors of the churches. Writing to Timothy, Paul says: "Do the work of an evangelist, make full proof of thy ministry." The full proof and fruitage of our ministry come only when we are true evangelists. A spiritual awakening does not depend upon vocational evangelists. They have their place, but as Bishop Theodore S. Henderson of the Methodist Church once said: "When evangelistic leadership departs from her pastors, Methodism's evangelistic power is gone." Nor does a spiritual awakening in America depend upon the evangelistic fervor of a few great churches but upon the revitalizing of innumerable churches, the largest and the smallest. There are no unimportant parishes.

In Hugh Walpole's book *Rogue Herries*, Francis Herries had just come into the desolate north of England in the early eighteenth century. Riding through the country he came upon a few buildings and there he met a shabby clergyman.

"How shall I find this place?" Herries asked. "Is it cut off from the world?"

The clergyman replied scornfully: "It is the world, sir. Here within these hills, in this space of ground is all the world. I thought while I was with my Lord Petersham that the world was there, but in every village through which I have passed since then I have found the complete world—all anger and vanity and covetousness and lust, yes, and all charity and goodness and sweetness of soul. But most of all here in this valley I have found the whole world. Lives are lived here completely without any thought of the countries more distant. You will find everything here, sir. God and the devil both walk on these fields." [2]

[1] By permission of The Bethany Press.
[2] Copyright 1930 by Doubleday & Company, Inc. Used by permission.

Our little sphere of service is an epitome of the whole earth—all heaven and hell are struggling there. We must each win the battle for righteousness in our own sector of the broad battle front.

The irresistible incoming of the mighty tide is related to innumerable individual waves and tiny ripples. They are all part of the movement of the tide, and spiritual awakening in tiny hamlets is essential to any national movement of spiritual refreshing. The glory of the spring is not a coverlet woven in heaven and laid down upon the earth, but glorious renewal beginning in innumerable tiny roots that find "a soul in grass and flowers."

It may seem to some more difficult to promote evangelism in our larger and more elaborate churches than in the smaller, less formal ones. In fact, in a recent evangelistic conference a young man asked: "How is it possible to have a vital evangelism against the background of the formal settings in our churches?" His question was a confession that we have allowed evangelism to be so long and exclusively associated with sawdust and trombones that we have forgotten that dignity and culture and evangelism and fervor are not mutually exclusive. There is, however, a warning in the young man's question, to which we may well give heed. Elaborate forms of worship may satisfy the needs of some natures. So long as there is vitality in the spiritual life of the church, a ritual of one sort or another may help to express that spirit. Too frequently, however, when spiritual fervor departs the ritual becomes a substitute for real spirituality. There is a tendency for forms to become elaborate in inverse ratio to the flow of spiritual devotion.

The same thing is true of preaching. When the heart is empty it may adorn itself with greater display; on the other hand, preaching need not be crude in order to be effectively evangelistic. Indeed most of our cultured preachers have been evangelistic, for evangelism is not marginal and peripheral but central and basic. The greatest preaching of the ages has been evangelistic, and although tabernacles and tents have frequently provided the setting for some modern evangelism, great cathedral-like churches have also supplied a fitting background for evangelism. Charles L. Goodell had a marvelous evangelistic ministry in the stately Calvary Methodist Church in New York City, and John Timothy Stone built the aristocratic Fourth Presbyterian Church, on the near North Side in Chicago, on evangelism. The elaborateness of great churches never seems to have proved a handicap to pastors with true evangelistic passion. Liturgical churches like the Church of England and the various branches of Lutheranism in the United States are now rousing themselves to evangelistic endeavor. John Wesley was never anything but an "immaculate, erudite Oxford don," whose speech was always classical English, and George Whitefield was also a typical English gentleman, cultured and refined. Yet they were among the most effective evangelists. There is no incompatibility between culture and the fervor ordinarily associated with effective evangelism. As a matter of fact we must add fervor to our present-day culture if we are to experience a spiritual awakening. In preparation for writing his pamphlet *The Sun Is Up* Franklin D. Elmer, Jr. wrote dozens of ministers, missionaries, and college presidents, asking what they felt to be the greatest hindrance to successful evangelism today. The answers came back almost unanimously: "The lethargy and indifference of Christians in the churches."

Preaching may restore Christians to the warmth of their early love for their Saviour, and it may rouse them to their responsibility and fire them with enthusiasm to win men for their Lord. If we are to have a spiritual awakening there must first be a rebirth of dynamic preaching in our pulpits. Someone has pointed out that Hinduism lives by ritual and social organization, Buddhism by meditation, Confucianism by a code of manners, but Christianity lives by "the foolishness of preaching." Whatever method is employed in soul winning, preaching creates the atmosphere in which it can be successfully accomplished. It sets the tone.

Like Francis of Assisi, Wesley reinstated the preacher. The Wesleyan revival was a revival of preaching. In the churches of that time sermons were delivered, but preaching in the true sense of the word hardly existed. Moral essays, innocent homilies, soulless platitudes, with a text attached to them, were droned out Sunday after Sunday from the various pulpits of the land, but preaching—the living message pouring from the living heart, appealing, warning, convicting—all that form of it was practically unknown. When, then, Whitefield and Wesley stood up; when their voices, thrilling with emotion, fell upon startled ears, men awoke, their hearts awoke, they realized their hunger and despair, they felt the first throbbings of a new and divine life stirring within them.[3]

Charles Jefferson once said concerning the preaching of his day:

Bright things, true things, helpful things are said in abundance, but the spiritual passion is lacking. The service smacks of time and not of eternity. The atmosphere of the sermon is not that of Mount Sinai or Mount Calvary, but that of the professor's room or the sanctum of the editor.

As Cecil Northcott of England says: "The fever does not get us."

President Eliot of Harvard once prophesied that the religion of the future would be intellectual and not emotional. His prophecy has been fulfilled to a great extent. Most of us have reacted too far from all emotion in our religious life and our pulpit ministry. As the train came to a stop in the station at Pittsburgh, a traveler was amused at the sign "Ice never fails." At least in some churches it is true that ice never fails. While the modern man abhors theatrical emotion in the pulpit obviously "worked up," yet he also despises icebergs in the pulpit and ice cubes in the pews. Says Paul Scherer: "To rely upon the emotions is demoralizing; to shun them is stupid and impossible," and then he quotes: "Moonlight preaching ripens no harvests." Herbert Spencer has said: "In the genesis of a system of thought the emotional nature is a large factor, perhaps as large a factor as the intellectual." Alexander Maclaren agrees:

[3] James Burns, *Revivals, Their Laws and Leaders*. By permission of James Clarke & Co., Ltd.

There is a kind of religious teachers who are always preaching down enthusiasm and preaching up what they call "sober standards of feeling" in matters of religion. By which, in nine cases out of ten, they mean precisely such a tepid condition as is described in much less polite language when the Voice from Heaven says, "Because thou art . . . neither cold nor hot, I will spue thee out of my mouth." I should have thought that the last piece of furniture which any Christian church in the nineteenth century needed was a refrigerator. A poker and a pair of bellows would be much more needful to them. Not to be all aflame is madness, if we believe our own creed.

Joseph Parker adds his powerful word:

As long as the church of God is one of many institutions, she will have her little day. She will die and that will be all. But just as soon as she gets the spirit of Jesus until the world thinks she has gone stark mad, then we shall be on the high road to capture this planet for Jesus.

Preachers of a living gospel need to let their hearers see their hearts. Cold intellectuality will never move men. In his book *Winning Men* John Timothy Stone says:

Sometimes, when I have been about to enter my pulpit, after coming directly from the small prayer circle of elders and from a prayer with the choir, I have felt utterly incapable of presenting the message of the morning, no matter how carefully it had been prepared. And I have made this silent prayer within the shrine of my own soul, "O Lord, give me heart. Let men see the love of God for the world this morning. Help me to give the true emotion of my soul to the Truth and Word. 'Speak to me that I may speak.' 'Open thou my lips that my mouth may show forth thy praise.' May there be the 'tongues of fire.' " We of our own mother church are too much afraid to show our hearts, and we become professional. What convinces the world if it is not the heart?

Said an old Puritan:

I marvel how I can preach stolidly and coldly, how I can let men alone in their sins, and that I do not go to them and beseech them

58

for the Lord's sake—however they take it and whatever pains or trouble it should cause me. When I come out of my pulpit I am not accused of want of ornaments or elegance, nor of letting fall an unhandsome word, but my conscience asketh me: "How could you speak of life and death with such a heart? How couldst thou preach of heaven and hell in such a careless and sleepy manner?" Truly this peal of the conscience doth ring in my ears: "O Lord, do that on our own souls that thou wouldst use us to do on the souls of others."[4]

I have a letter yellow with age, a letter written by Bishop Theodore S. Henderson to his pastors, in which he says:

You have poured out your soul to God for your people. But I press the question—it needs pressing—it must have an answer. There will be no revival without it. Here it is. God search us as we ask it and answer it. *Have I poured out my soul to my people for Christ's sake in the same way that I have poured out my soul to God for my people's sake?* Have the people seen your concern? Have they heard the quaver in your voice? Have they witnessed any pallor in your face? Do they know that you would rather have a genuine revival than anything else and all else God has to give? If there is any doubt of it, form that inner circle and pour out your soul to them. Keep pouring out your soul until you are: "forspent, forspent." *Let your church and community know about your spiritual concern for others* just as God knows about it. Then the revival will come. *It will come, not by organization, but by communication.*

The preacher may make his pulpit a King Tut's tomb, ornamented with the jewels of antiquity, words and phrases that flashed with meaning in a past generation but which have little appeal for the present day, but he is only ornamenting the dead. His pulpit still remains a tomb. Jewels do not flash in darkness. The preacher may repeat word for word the sermons of Savonarola, Beecher, or Phillips Brooks, and they will fall upon dead ears unless he shows people his own passionate heart in his message.

[4] Quoted by Charles L. Goodell in *Heralds of a Passion.*

When permission to print one of his sermons was once asked of George Whitefield he said: "I have no objection if you will print the lightning, thunder, and rainbow with it." Without the passion of a God-intoxicated personality and the "lightning, thunder, and rainbow" of a soul-moving concern for the salvation of men, and awesome consciousness of the majesty of a holy God revealing his wrath against all unrighteousness and sin, and a glowing heart rejoicing in the revelation of a righteousness of God through an atoning Saviour, even the great sermons of the princes of the pulpit will be like an empty armor standing in a great hall no longer throwing fear into the hearts of enemies or inspiring followers because there is no living knight in the armor. Bishop William Fraser McDowell said: "A fine woman came home from one of the finest churches in New York and said: 'It was well enough in every respect save one: it did not matter.'"

It was at Pentecost that the church was empowered to conquer the mighty Roman Empire, which had itself conquered the whole world. The symbol of Pentecost was a flame, and the symbol of the true evangelist is a flame. Whitefield's tomb has a flaming heart carved upon it, and the symbol on Adam Clark's grave is a candle burned down to the socket, under which is the inscription: "In living for others I am burned away." If "the combustible materials for a glorious conflagration are here," let us heed the word of Paul to Timothy: "Stir into a flame the gift of God which is in thee." Men are not saved by technique or eloquence but through the contagion of a glowing heart. I have referred to a letter Bishop Theodore S. Henderson wrote years ago. In it he said:

At the close of an address before a ministers' meeting, one of the ministers came forward and asked me if I had time to listen to a story. "Certainly," I replied, "tell me." I can give only in brief what he told me.

"Many years ago," he said, "there came into our home a bundle of heaven in the form of a big, wholesome, healthy baby boy. There was no evidence that he was not in perfect health. But when he was about three years old a subtle disease fastened itself upon him. All

60

that the family doctor could do availed nothing. Then he suggested a consultation with a specialist. We followed instructions faithfully. The specialist was baffled. He could do nothing more than our family physician. We brought our baby home and watched him grow thinner and paler every day. One day, when the physician was present, he reached for the baby's pulse and it was gone. He listened for the heart beat and it was not there. Then the baby's eyes fluttered; his eyes grew glassy; and the little chin dropped. 'The baby is dead,' said the doctor as kindly as he could. Any parent can imagine the stab of that hour. But I could not give him up. I called to my wife to bring the warm blankets. I tore open my clothing; I lifted the limp form of my baby and put him over my heart; my wife wrapped us up in the blankets. I held my baby there nine hours."

For a few seconds the minister's lips quivered and he said: "My baby is now twenty-three years old, a senior in college, and is doing a wonderful work for Christ."

I stood aghast as I looked at him. His boy had been saved by a glowing heart.

It is the prophet who puts his face to the face of the widow's child, his heart to the child's heart, who brings the dead to life for only from the warmth of a flaming soul are other souls warmed. The blood of transfusion must be warm with life. Years ago my friend Bishop Ralph Cushman told a story which came to life in his book *The Essentials of Evangelism*:

I have never forgotten the question that Leslie Weatherhead of London asked the ministers of Greater New York a few years ago. I got the story the next day from a friend, a distinguished minister in New York. Weatherhead's ship was late in getting into New York harbor. The crowd of ministers that packed Fifth Avenue Presbyterian Church waited long for his coming. My friend went down in a tug to meet the distinguished Englishman. When at last they got him into the church, and he stood up to speak, he said: "I have three questions to ask you," and these New York ministers listened with somewhat of amazement to the first question, which was: 'Do you have it? My brethren, do you have it?' A strange question for a distinguished London preacher to ask a group of American ministers! But the preacher went on to explain: "Do you have the experience of the reality of the Presence of the living Christ in your life? Do you know the power and the joy of this Presence?" Then he went on: "You may have all else, culture, brilliance, education, but if you do not have this, the joy of his Presence, if he is not a reality to you, then you will be a failure as a minister of the gospel of Jesus Christ." [5]

We must preach the gospel out of the Bible, but we must also preach it out of the depths of our own inner selves, out of our own convictions and experiences. The gospel we preach is a revelation of God, but it is also a revelation of the experience of God's grace and power in ourselves. If Christ is not the answer in our own case we shall not be able to present him with any real conviction as the answer to the world's needs. If he has not satisfied the deepest longings of our own souls we cannot fervently present him as the satisfaction for the needs of others. In an article which appeared in the *British Weekly* James Reid said:

It is the feeling we give others that we have found victory over the world and can tell them the secret, that is the great need; and therefore it is something more than just vague sympathy. If we never find others seeking our help, we should ask ourselves if we really care about people. Above all else, we should ask if we *ourselves* know that experience of victory in life for which many behind the mask of cheerfulness are seeking.

Weatherhead asked the first and most important question: "Do you have it?" There is another important question: "Can you impart it?"

John Wesley wondered that no layman or minister helped to bring him into the light, when for years he was seeking the way. William Law was one of those ministers. Wesley later wrote him: "How will you answer to our common Lord that you, sir, never led me into the light? Why did I scarcely ever hear you name the *name of Christ?* Why did you never urge

* By permission of the General Board of Evangelism, The Methodist Church.

me to *faith in his blood?* Is not Christ the First and the Last? If you say that you thought I had faith already, verily, you know nothing of me. I beseech you, sir, by the mercies of God, to consider whether the true reason of your never pressing this salvation upon me was not this—that you never had it yourself!" *Many a minister has since read that letter on his knees* as he searched his own heart to discover whether he has been guilty of not making clear to the people who listen to him how a man can get right with God and live in fellowship with him.

True evangelistic preaching is characterized by courage and clarity. It is not frozen in the ice of dogmatic rigidity. When ministers experience spiritual awakening they are freed from the dead letter of the law. At other times they may spend their time in the pulpit attempting to defend the faith, prove the doctrines of the church, or debate dogmas as zealously as the Popes of Rome strove to maintain traditional dogmas, even when the sense of vitality out of which these doctrines were born had departed from them, leaving them like shells along the shore, shells from which all life had so long since departed that they were empty and dry. With a new baptism of the spirit such as comes in times of spiritual awakening, the pulpit speaks the living message of the word of God in its relevancy to the needs of men's souls and the needs of the day. Then men are freed from the false conception of tolerance that makes them apologetic and hesitant in preaching. The pulpit dares to make great claims for Christ and preaches his cross and atonement with no uncertain sound. Christ is preached instead of a general and vague Christian ethics. Humanism is revealed as shallow and dated as compared with the timely timelessness of the gospel. There is a sharper cutting edge on preaching and, as a result, a new daring assurance and aggressiveness about Christianity. A new sense of urgency creeps into the preacher's soul when a spiritual awakening is in the making, and increases when the awakening becomes a recognized fact, an urgency that is at once communicated to his people. There is need of decision; admiring Christ and proving his teaching is not enough now. The pulpit sounds the new-old note, "Choose you this day whom ye will serve." Along with the note of urgency there is born a sense of expectancy. At other times preachers often go into their pulpits with the idea of conducting the "usual services." They mount the pulpit steps obsessed with the idea that nothing is going to happen and naturally nothing does happen. A young minister once asked Charles Haddon Spurgeon why it was that though he preached faithfully no one was ever converted. The great London preacher asked: "You don't expect people to be converted at every service, do you?"

"No, of course not," replied the young man.

"That is exactly why they are not converted," commented Spurgeon.

When a spiritual awakening comes ministers are constantly expectant and their faith is rewarded.

VI

The Impregnable Rock

MEN WORKING ON A ROAD GANG were eating their lunch by the side of the road. A rabbit jumped out of the brush and sat up curiously surveying the intruders. A young man born in China asked the foreman: "Do you want to see me catch that rabbit?" The foreman laughingly said "Yes," certain in his own mind that he could not do it. The young man took his hat in one hand and his gloves in the other. Creeping up on the rabbit he threw one glove on one side of it and then quickly threw the other glove on the other side. The little creature was so confused, not knowing which way to turn, that he sat stock-still. The boy threw his hat over him and captured him. Revolutionary changes come into the modern world with just such lightning rapidity. So many voices call him, so many movements claim his loyalty, so many conflicting ideologies and panaceas, each insisting that it is the only way out, that the modern man sits down in the midst of the welter bewildered, unable to decide what is true, and which is the way to go. A materialistic education has confused young minds; nor is the bewilderment confined to youth. A member of Congress said recently: "We do not laugh at the other political party because it does not know what to do now that it is in control, for we remember that when we were in control we did not know what to do either."

There has been confusion in the pulpit as well as in business, government, and education. A minister stopped where two boys were playing and asked: "Could either of you boys tell me the way to the post office?"

One of the boys said: "Sure, just a block down the street there."

The minister paused a moment and said: "By the way, why

don't you come to Sunday school and let me teach you the way to heaven?"

One of the boys said: "Teach us the way to heaven! You didn't even know the way to the post office."

Ministers have long been called sky pilots. When one steps into an airplane he wants to be assured the pilot knows his plane and the way to take him safely through the air and put him down at the port. But long has the message of the pulpit been halting and uncertain because many ministers were not sure of their ground. Historical and literary criticism made them hesitate to speak with clear conviction regarding the cardinal doctrines of the faith. The result has been that the pulpit has frequently evaded the great truths of the Word of God, and as a substitute, preaching has concerned itself with magnifying "certain desirable qualities of character." Ethical instructions are important, but they are not a substitute for the eternal facts of sin, salvation, God, Christ, and eternal life. Is it not true that our evangelism has been too nebulous? A generation has been received into many of our churches without positive convictions; and the membership of the churches by and large is ignorant of the sublime truths of the Word of God. Some ministers have preached a gospel with about as much nourishment in it as one would receive if he walked through a London fog with his mouth open. Men are not attracted by a condensed fog. Even theological professors proclaimed themselves for "the good life," without defining any more than other philosophers had done what they meant by "the good life." Because the sharp distinction and clearly defined message of Christianity has not been sounded with a note of certainty, men have left the church believing it to be little more helpful than the country club or the lodge.

We have now passed through the period of testing and uncertainty. Everything vital in the Christian message has gone through the fire and emerged unscathed. Our message is now stronger and more certain because of the trial by fire. The evangelism of the new day must have more vital content and be based upon great scripture truth. Doubt is never magnetic.

Charles L. Goodell once told of a little bronze statue he saw in an art shop in Paris. It was a statue of a knight of olden times, clad in linked mail. His good sword was at his side. His pose was one of conscious strength and his face was aglow with intensity of purpose. He held before him a scroll which bore for its legend the single word "Credo." It is only when a man can say "I believe" that he amounts to much in awakening faith in other men. We must believe mightily, and we must have confidence in our weapons. In the armory of the Earl of Pembroke it is said that there are corselets which show that the arrows of the English used to go through the breastplate, through the body of the warrior, and out through the backplate.

We need to remember that the King's arrows are sharp in the hearts of his enemies, that the sturdy bow of the gospel has shot the arrow of conviction to the hearts of men in times past. We must believe that again the great verses of scripture, like polished shafts, can fly to the souls of men and that the Word of God is a quiver full of such shafts. The gospel has in it power to pardon every sin, heal every wound, correct every wrong, cure every trouble, emancipate every slave, ransom every nation, and bring every man to heaven.

Charles G. Finney said that a revival results from the proclamation of some formerly neglected truth of the Word of God. There are rich veins of pure gold in the Scriptures never yet mined by the mind of man, truths that can break like living light upon the bewildered mind of our civilization. Joan of Arc said to her judges: "My Lord God hath a book in which are written many things which the most learned clerk and scholars have never come across." The outstanding truths emphasized during the Reformation had become tarnished by time and fallen into disuse in the days before Jonathan Edwards and Whitefield in America and Wesley in England. A hopeless sort of fatalism, almost as dark as the cloud of modern despair, had settled upon the people, a deistic belief in the separation of God from his world, the predestination of certain privileged people to eternal life, and the inevitable damnation of all others,

67

left the people hopeless and aimless. Of what value was virtue? Why follow after righteousness if, on the one hand, the good things of this life and, on the other hand, the promise of life eternal, were only for a privileged class? France crowned a prostitute Goddess of Reason and England exalted reason above revelation. Redemption through simple faith in Christ had been obscured by the idea of salvation through the sacraments of the church. Although it stems from the scientific ideas of our age rather than hyper-Calvinistic teachings, our fatalism and despair are even greater than that of eighteenth-century England. The world believes we are in the grip of blind forces of unbelievable power bringing us toward our doom,

> And that inverted Bowl they call the Sky,
> Whereunder crawling coop'd we live and die,
>   Lift not your hands to *It* for help—for It
> As impotently moves as you or I.

The great evangelical awakening restored the lost emphasis upon ageless evangelical truths of scripture and brought hope to a hopeless people.

If we would change our country, as the great evangelical awakening changed England, we must return to the cardinal truths of the Word of God. No pretty little preachments on "certain desirable qualities of character" can transform men. The Augean stable cannot be cleansed by sprinkling rose water over it. Martin Luther said: "A man's heart is like some foul stable; wheelbarrows and shovels are of little use except to remove some of the surface filth and to litter all the passages in the process. What is to be done with it? Turn the Elbe into it. The floods will sweep away all the pollution." Only the mighty tides of God's grace in Christ can cleanse a man. Only that mighty river that flows from the Word of God can cleanse the life of a nation.

A man from the Middle West took his first plane trip of a few hours. When he came down his friends were disappointed that his reactions were so commonplace. They asked him how it felt to be up in the air. He said: "Oh, all right, but I'll tell you fellows one thing, all the time I was up there I never let my heft down once." Many a preacher has been afraid to be simple and direct in his preaching, to let his heft down on the broad, buoyant wings of the Word of God. Perhaps our experiences are commonplace, and our hearers' reactions are commonplace, because we have not surrendered ourselves to great and eternal truths. When one first rides in an airplane he is surprised by the mighty power of the giant motors lifting him above the earth up into a new freedom and exaltation. When the minister who has labored to prepare messages scholarly, eloquent, arresting, and perhaps ingenious, lets down his heft upon the mighty compelling power of great scripture truth, he rejoices in a new sense of authority and assurance. He is aware of kinship with the prophets of old. The tremendous impact of the Scriptures is in his speech. He is in tune with the Infinite, and he speaks to men's hearts. There is a new timelessness, a cosmic sweep in that particular pulpit. The man is above the temporal and the passing fashions of men's thoughts. He is no longer bound by their philosophies. He then knows that we do not make the gospel great by proclaiming it. Rather the gospel makes us great when we preach it.

The prophets, the apostles, the church fathers, the reformers, the mighty preachers of history, were made great by the great evangel which flowed through their souls and their personalities to the people. Savonarola preached in Florence until he had emptied his church. Then, like Paul going into Arabia, he went to a monastery in Bologna, where he pored over the Scriptures. In them he discovered a message adequate to the needs of his day. When he had laid hold upon the message of the Word of God, no building in Florence was large enough to hold the crowds that came to hear him.

Let me show you three pictures. The first hangs in the library at Erfurt. In it a Roman Catholic monk is shown in that very library poring over a book for which he had hungered as men long without food hunger for bread. He had never heard the Bible properly expounded. There, in the library, Luther came upon certain words that Bishop Lightfoot insisted represent "the concentration and epitome of all revealed religion—The just shall live by faith."

The setting of the second picture is the Benedictine convent at Bologna. The same monk, who has now crossed the Alps, is sick, so sick that he fears he is going to die, to die in a foreign land. Utter darkness—hopeless! His sins! Judgment! His mind is filled with fear and dread. Then those words, those magic words that were to change the course of history and make the world over, come to him like a light from heaven: "The just shall live by faith."

The third picture shows the monk on a staircase, Pilate's staircase, somehow miraculously transported from Jerusalem to Rome. The pope has promised indulgences to those who ascend Pilate's staircase on their knees. As the monk makes his painful way up the stairs, words come to him, words he heard in the library and in the convent years before, great words from the Word of God, from Paul's letter to the Romans, "The just shall live"—not by ridiculous superstitions—"the just shall live by faith." These are the words that changed the world, the words out of which Protestantism was born. Whether or not these three poetic pictures represent the sober facts of history, they fittingly epitomize Luther's growing understanding of the basic and essential concept of salvation by faith rather than by ritual—the evangelical conception.

That was 1517. Two centuries pass. England is "ripe for disintegration and chaos." A priest of the Church of England has returned from a mission to the Indians of Georgia, which proved a dismal failure. He says: "What have I learned? Why, I have learned what I least of all suspected, that I, who went to America to convert the Indians, was never myself converted to God!" One day early in 1738, he is chatting with three of his friends when all at once they begin to speak of their faith, the faith that leads to pardon, the faith that links a man with God, the faith that brings joy and peace through believing. Was there such a religion as that? Could such a faith be his? he asks his companions. They replied that this faith was the gift, the free gift of God, and that God would surely bestow it upon every soul who earnestly and perseveringly sought it. Wesley made up his mind that it should be his. "I resolved to seek it unto the end," he says.

Augustus Spangenberg, a Moravian pastor, asked him: "Do you know Jesus Christ?"

"I know," replied Wesley, after an awkward pause. "I know that he is the Saviour of the world."

"True," answered the Moravian, "but do you know that he has saved *you*?"

"I hope he has died to save me," Wesley responded.

The Moravian asked one more question: "Do you know yourself?"

"I said that I did," Wesley said, "but I fear they were vain words!"

He saw others happy, rejoicing in a faith that seemed to transfigure their lives. What was it that was *theirs* and yet not *his*? "Are they read in philosophy?" he asks. "So was I. In ancient or modern tongues? So was I also. Are they versed in the science of divinity? I too have studied it many years. Can they talk fluently upon spiritual things? I could do the same. Are they plenteous in alms? Behold I give all my goods to feed the poor! I have laboured more abundantly than they all. I have thrown up my friends, reputation, ease, country; I have put my life in my hand, wandering into strange lands; I have given my body to be devoured by the deep, parched up with heat, consumed by toil and weariness. But does all this make me acceptable to God! Does all this make me a Christian? By no means! I have sinned and come short of the glory of God. I am alienated from the life of God. I am a child of wrath. I have no hope."

An Episcopal rector who knew he did not properly believe on the Saviour thrilled a ministers' meeting in a Middle Western city one Monday morning when he announced: "Brethren, I have found Christ. I have been ministering in the church for years, but I did not know him. I found him yesterday as I walked on the hills above the city. Now all is changed."

So it was with Wesley when, very much against his will, he attended the historic meeting in Aldersgate Street. As in the case of Luther, it was the Epistle to the Romans through which was revealed to him the way of salvation through faith. In fact it was while someone was reading Luther's preface to the Epistle to the Romans, Wesley says,

About a quarter before nine, while he was describing the change which God works in the heart through faith in Christ, I felt my heart strangely warmed. I felt I did trust in Christ alone, for my salvation; and an assurance was given me that He had taken away my sins, even mine, and saved me from the law of sin and death.

From that experience Wesley went forth to preach "salvation by faith," as a vital, personal experience, and the "priesthood of all believers." The "open Bible" became a guide to daily life and conduct.

The American revival at about this time was also a revival of the Bible. Jonathan Edwards, the outstanding preacher of the period, like Luther and Wesley, made justification by faith, the message of the Epistle to the Romans, the central doctrine of his crusade.

The fires of the Revival had been kindled from heaven, and before the accession of George III the Congregational churches had caught the flame. Their ministers were beginning to preach with a new fervor, and their preaching was followed by a new success. The religious life of the people was becoming more intense. A passion for evangelistic work had taken possession of church after church, and by the end of the century the old Meeting Houses were crowded; many had to be enlarged and new ones had to be erected in town after town, and village after village, in every part of the country.[1]

A similar thing happened when Robert Haldane came to Geneva, where John Calvin had wrought heroically and suc-

[1] *This Freedom—Whence?* by J. Wesley Bready. By permission of the American Tract Society.

cessfully. Now, however, Unitarianism had set aside the Bible as a textbook in the theological seminary. With some of the students Haldane

commenced a systematic study of the Epistle to the Romans. Here they were at once confronted with a terrible truth which flatly contradicted their accepted teaching, the truth of man's depravity, his impotence, his utter sinfulness. Gathering all the force of scripture on this great fundamental, he earnestly pressed home the truth until the awakened conscience gave full assent to it. Then what he had hoped and prayed for came to pass. A very beautiful thing happened. The merely intellectual thirst for knowledge changed into a deep spiritual concern. The theological class became a class of anxious inquirers! How eagerly now did they follow the exposition of the great epistle as their teacher passed on to the grand disclosure of the grace of God in the gospel! [2]

Page after page of history points to the Epistle to the Romans as the book of revivals. The twentieth-century revival for which we pray may not come through this particular book, but if it does come it will come, as have all other revivals in history, through prayer and a new discovery and preaching of the Scriptures. For regardless of the godlessness of the age and the unbelief among men, there is a deep and general popular sense of the authority of the Bible. A true and telling evangelistic sermon is not completely given over to exhortation. It must teach and instruct, and the teaching will be in the great truths of the Word of God. The evangelism of the past generation has been too nebulous. There must be more content in the evangelism of the future. It must be based upon the Scriptures. Yet it will not arrest the attention or challenge the age if it is a mere verbal repetition of passages of Holy Writ or a platitudinous paraphrase of Scripture. It must lay bare to the eyes of this generation the essential meaning of these passages, and so apply the universal teachings of the Word of God to our times, and interpret the situations that formed the settings of Bible passages in terms of contemporary life

[2] *Old-Time Revivals.*

situations that the pressing urgency these teachings had when first presented may explode upon the present generation like the unexpected thunder of a storm, or burst upon the people with the fresh surprise of a morning sunrise.

To move our age preaching must be gripping. Preachers must not "pull their punches" but speak frankly of men's sins and confidently of Christ's power to forgive and cure sin. The sermon must grip because it is clear and understandable to the people who hear it. A knowledge of biblical truth is not enough for the preachers of the new age. They must also know people and speak their language. A leading lawyer in New York said: "Half the time I don't know what my preacher is talking about."

A young man teaching his primary class in Sunday school said: "Jesus wept." Then he paused and asked the boys if they knew what that meant. They didn't.

He said: "That means Jesus cried."

A six-year-old boy spoke up: "Why didn't you say that in the first place?"

I once flew from North Dakota to keep a speaking engagement in Philadelphia. There was a strong head wind, and it became apparent that we would not make a plane connection in New York. The plane would not stop in Philadelphia. We flew over the city. I was ready, but up above the city, unable to get down to the people to deliver my message. It is unfortunate when a minister cannot get down to the level of his people. The common people, on the other hand, heard Jesus gladly because he dealt with the profoundest themes in such simple terms that they understood and believed. That "immaculate, erudite Oxford don" John Wesley, whose speech was always classical English, was heard, understood, and accepted by the humblest people of England. He marvelously influenced for God "soldiers, sailors, publicans, miners, fishermen, smugglers, and the roughest industrial workers." Let no man despise the preachers who make the truth simple and clear to the common people. There is much more art in that than in the ability to mouth high-sounding philosophical terms

74

acquired in college and theological classrooms. Said Principal Denney: "The man who shoots above the target does not prove thereby that he has superior ammunition. He just proves that he can't shoot." "It is with words as with sunbeams—the more they are condensed, the deeper they burn." Truth must first be clear to the preacher before he can put it in such terms as will make it lucid to the people in his audiences. It is when the preacher sees truth clearly and feels it deeply that it moves his hearers. Make it plain and press it upon men.

Let us remember that we have not evangelized when we have merely opened the evangel to view. We have not evangelized when we have "confronted men with the gospel." We only evangelize when we press the claims of Christ upon men and, with gentle but insistent and persistent compulsion, persuade them to taste and see that the Lord is good, and partake of the rich feast provided by divine grace. By all means give an invitation to men to accept Christ and join the church after each sermon. When one's friend says, "Come to dinner sometime," one usually does not go. On the other hand, when a friend says, "Will you have dinner with us tonight at six o'clock?" if one has no other engagement and wants to dine with the friend, one usually goes. It is natural that men will not respond when they are not invited, or invited very casually to sometime accept Christ and unite with his church. But when a minister says, "Come to Christ. Come now," men are likely to respond. A line in the church calendar below the announcement of the closing invitation hymn will help—"The doors of the church are open at all services. Those desiring membership are cordially invited to come forward and present themselves." When the closing hymn is announced the minister may add a personal word to the invitation in the church bulletin: "This is our hymn of invitation. Those present who wish to confess Christ as their Saviour, or any who desire to unite with our church in any way we receive members, will please come forward as we sing this hymn." Let the minister come down from the pulpit and stand in the front of the sanctuary while the hymn is being sung, thus indicating his confidence that people will respond to the invitation. There may not always be a response, and if there is none there need be no embarrassment and no sense of defeat. The hymn ended, the benediction may be pronounced at once. There is little need of continuing the invitation for any great length of time when it is extended at every service, except when there is a continuing response; then it may be well to add a further word: "Are there others who will come now and stand by the side of these who have declared themselves for Christ and the church? We pause a moment before the closing prayer and benediction that you may join us."

When people come forward, if the minister does not know them, he may speak quietly to each of them while the congregation is singing, thus discovering whether they are coming to make profession of their faith in Christ for the first time or to bring their membership from another church. He may then announce to the congregation: "Mr. and Mrs. Walter Wilson, now members of Calvary Church in Buffalo, have presented themselves for membership in our church. Their coming will be a blessing to us, and we hope our fellowship will also prove a blessing to them. When their church letters of transfer have been received they will be formally welcomed into our church." Of course procedures of various denominations will differ somewhat at this point.

When many are expected to respond to the invitation at a service, some person may be designated in advance to pass cards and pencils among them and then hand the cards to the minister for announcement. The proper co-operation of the congregation in this procedure is almost as important as the conduct of the minister. At a recent meeting of the Northern Baptist Convention, President E. T. Dahlberg referred to "postdoxologist" Baptists and "prebenedictionist" Baptists. He explained that by postdoxologists he meant those who come into the service after the doxology has been sung, and by prebenedictionists he meant those who reach for their wraps and get ready to leave the church while the invitation is being extended. By such action worshipers may defeat the purpose of the invitation. By secret prayer and devotional participation in the invitation hymn they may help to win men to Christ. They may help also by greeting those who respond to the call. Where the invitation is given regularly members of the church soon form the habit of going to shake the hands of the new people and to express their pleasure at their coming into the church. Sometimes they will already know them; often they come from churches or towns in which they themselves once lived, and bonds of friendship are formed at once. Those who come to the front of the church to confess their faith for the first time may be taken into the study or vestry at the close of the service for instructions and prayer. Certainly the pastor should call within the week on all those who have responded to the invitation.

VII

Curbstones and Doorsteps

IT IS SAID that after he had been in office only four days President Franklin D. Roosevelt called upon ninety-two-year-old Justice Oliver Wendell Holmes, who had retired from the Supreme Court. President Roosevelt asked Justice Holmes, who served as a soldier during the Civil War: "What is your advice to me?"

"Mr. President," he replied, "you're in a war. I've been in a war. There is only one thing to do in a war. Form your battalions and carry the fight to the enemy."

He referred to a different kind of war from that in which the United States was later plunged, but that is good advice in any war. It was the strategy of the last conflict. In World War I the earth was slashed and the doughboys remained in fixed positions in the trenches, sometimes for long months at a time; but in World War II the idea of lightning war had taken hold, and the army made use of mobile units, self-propelled guns and tanks. The new strategy of Christian warfare should likewise lay emphasis upon mobility rather than fixity, going to the people where they are, rather than remaining in our church buildings and waiting for the people to come to us. This was the grand strategy of the great Captain of our salvation, who commanded his followers to "go out into the highways and hedges."

In one Protestant denomination it is said you do not have a church unless you also have a branch or mission. When I was pastor in a town of a thousand population, with a church of 250 members, I developed four Sunday schools in rural areas besides the school housed in the church. The other Sunday schools met in schoolhouses. Each Sunday afternoon I visited one of these Sunday schools and occasionally held a prayer meeting on a week night in the schoolhouse. Thirty new members were received into the church on profession of faith in one year from one of these branch Sunday schools. The most neglected areas in the country probably are the rural sections nearest to towns and cities. A young woman said of her preacher-father: "His greatest sermons were not preached in the pulpit but when he was out fishing, tramping through the woods, or sitting on a log down by the side of the lake." In that he was like his Master. Jesus did preach in the synagogues, but he was most at home speaking from a fisherman's boat, pushed out a little from the land, or in the fields. He was a great after-dinner speaker and some of his greatest discourses were delivered at the friendly table. Some ministers deliver their best sermons at outdoor meetings, factories, colleges, labor unions, luncheon clubs, lodges, or social and fraternal gatherings. Of course at such times it is easy to yield to the temptation to become a mere entertainer, but under such circumstances the man with a message can often deliver it to a new and most appreciative audience. The minister will do well to seek and accept as many invitations as possible to address groups outside his church.

Says James Burns in *Revivals, Their Laws and Leaders*:

Wesley realized also the profound truth that it is not the duty of the Church to wait within the Church until the people come to it, but that it is the duty of the Church to go to the people. When on that day at Bristol, standing at Whitefield's side, he looked down upon that vast sea of upturned faces—the unpitied progeny of the streets, the lapsed and neglected masses of the people whom no one loved or cared for—the call came to him to separate himself from all the habits and conventional beliefs in which he had been trained, and discarding all ecclesiastical forms, deal directly with human needs. The struggle which followed was intense, as we have seen, for Wesley had been trained from his infancy to regard ecclesiastical forms and order with a veneration bordering upon awe. But stronger than all these inherited prejudices was the recognition in him of the divine will, and the power of absolute submission possessed only by the greatest natures. In the presence of that mute

79

but infinitely pathetic appeal which came to him from the up-turned faces of that awe-struck crowd, his prejudices withered within him; pity and love awoke in his heart, and made him willing to suffer all things if only he could win them for Christ.

Thus was begun that informal ministry which kept him all his life long wandering from place to place, preaching in the streets, by the roadside, anywhere, indeed, and at any time, if only he could get men to listen. And slowly the people began to awake to the fact that some strange thing was happening in their midst. This informal ministry began to stir into life the dormant spiritual forces of the nation. At first it aroused curiosity in all, then in many bitterness and persecution, but in others a strange joy. To the poor, at last, was the gospel being preached; to the outcasts and the abandoned once again was the glad offer of salvation made, and into the open doors of that gracious kingdom where the penitent and the needy are made welcome, they began to stream—first by ones and twos, next by hundreds, at last by thousands, until the whole land was filled with the song of the redeemed.[1]

One American minister has said that some preachers are like the great guns in their concrete emplacements along a coast. The guns rise up. There is a great burst of orange flame, and and then they disappear behind their emplacements. The minister rises up in the pulpit, there is a great burst of orange oratory, and then the minister disappears until next Sunday, when he reappears to deliver another shot. But a minister has not fulfilled his function when he has preached on Sunday from his remote pulpit. Daniel Webster once said: "If a lawyer were perched as high in the air and as far off from the jury as the minister was from his people a century ago he would not win a case in a lifetime." But one needs even closer contact with the people than that which the modern pulpit offers to win men to Christ. If it is true that we have not evangelized until we have urged the claims of Christ upon men, then it is our responsibility to get to the individual. This was Jesus' favorite approach. When Julia Ward Howe invited Charles Sumner to meet a distinguished guest at her house,

[1] By permission of James Clarke & Co., Ltd.

he replied: "I do not know that I wish to meet your friend. I have outlived my interest in individuals." Recording in her diary that night the senator's remark, Mrs. Howe wrote: "God Almighty, by latest accounts, had not got so far as this." Jesus was interested in individuals and he won them because they knew he loved them. Seven out of the eleven apostles were won through personal contact.

Let us never forget that we do not save souls in bundles. Henry Clay Trumbull, who was a master of great assemblies, wrote a little time before his death:

Looking back upon my work in all these years I can see more direct results of good through my individual efforts with individuals than I can know of through all my spoken words to thousands upon thousands of persons in religious assemblies, or all my written words on the pages of periodicals or of books. Reaching one person at a time is the best way of reaching all the world in time.

In his Yale lectures on preaching Dr. Burton said: "It has been the sin of my life that I have not always taken aim. I have been a lover of subjects. If I had loved men more, and loved subjects only as God's instrument of good for men, it would have been better and I should have more to show for my labor under the sun."

A story is told of an old man in the South who sat on the porch all day firing his shotgun. He never seemed to aim at anything; he just fired one shot after the other. Finally the neighbors sent for a doctor to examine him. The doctor asked him why he sat on the porch and fired his shotgun into space. He said: "Well, there are three objectives: one is to purify the atmosphere; the second is to drive away the devil; and the third, I might perhaps bring down a stray coon." Much preaching is like that, a shot at random with the hope that it may purify the atmosphere, drive away the devil, and possibly reach some soul; but a ministry to individuals, when the minister has "taken aim," gives him more to show for his "labor under the sun." As a matter of fact, great preachers

81

have almost uniformly been great personal workers. Moody and Spurgeon were made powerful in the pulpit because they dealt constantly with individuals. Spurgeon probably could not have averaged one convert a day for forty years if he had not dealt with individuals.

The old vicar who preceded Richard Baxter at Kidderminster preached only once a quarter and "then so foolishly that he roused only the laughter of his audience, while his curate was a drunkard seldom out of the alehouse," and the people were in gross spiritual darkness. But Baxter preached "as a dying man to dying men," and soon the great church was filled to overflowing and they had to add gallery after gallery to it. Yet the secret of his success was largely the fact that during the week he exhausted all his energy and time in trying to save the souls of his people one by one. He gathered them in groups; he formed them into classes; he dealt with them family by family; he appealed—earnestly, pleadingly, yearningly—to each individual alone. He arranged that every family in his parish should come to his house, one by one, and with each family he spent an hour. Then he took each member aside and urgently, tenderly, besought him to make immediate decision for Christ.

One of the items mentioned in the Lord's bill of particulars in his complaint against the pastors of Israel was that the shepherds had scattered the flock because they had not visited them. By way of contrast, Paul, giving an account of his stewardship at Ephesus, says: "I . . . have taught you publicly, and from house to house."

We have often applied the figure of fishing to soul winning. Fishermen go where the fish are. If there are few people in our churches, the streets, the parks and public places are full of them. Why should we not think of the minister as like Nimrod, "A mighty hunter before the Lord"—one who hunts men. The hunter does not go to Times Square in New York or State and Madison Streets in Chicago, expecting to see a pheasant rise from the covert of the subway kiosk, or a deer spring across the lobby of the McAlpin or the Morrison

82

Hotel. The hunter goes into the wilds, far from the beaten paths. Nor can mighty hunters before the Lord hunt from cushioned pulpits and comfortable church pews. We shall have to exchange our robes for the saddlebags of Wesley and the stirrups of David Brainerd. If we would win people we must go to them where they are.

"I've always believed in miracles, but I never believed this one could happen," said a woman to her pastor. When she had announced her intention of uniting with the church by letter, the pastor inquired about her son and her husband who had attended services with her. As far as one could discover, however, no one had ever made an earnest effort to interest them. After a brief talk with the son at the church door the minister secured his decision for Christ and the church. He then made an appointment to see the husband at his home. There was one appeal to make, an appeal that reaches every true parent's heart, the appeal of the children. The pastor began by saying: "I'm so glad you are coming to church with your family. You have a great boy. He has made a deep impression upon me. You must be very proud of him. You know your wife and your boy are meeting the deacons on Thursday night to confess Christ and unite with the church. Wouldn't it be a wonderful thing if that boy could always remember that when he declared himself for Christ his father was by his side? Wouldn't it be a great help to him if, when he was baptized, his father was with him?" Little did the pastor know then that within two years that boy would be beyond the blue waters of the Pacific, far from home and exposed to fierce temptations, and that the father, a strong man, would be stricken with an incurable illness while the boy was at war.

The wife had said: "He is not interested." But that is no way to approach a man. Instead the minister said: "I am sure you are interested."

"Of course I am interested," he replied. "Everyone is interested in that, but no one ever put it up to me like that before. I can't answer you now."

83

The pastor was wise enough to say: "I'm not asking you to give your answer now, but Thursday night your wife and your boy will present themselves for church membership. Give me your answer then."

On Thursday evening the man brought his wife and his son to the church in the car. He threw his overcoat over a back pew and followed his family into the pastor's study. When the wife and son had given their statement of faith to the board of deacons, the pastor turned to the husband and asked: "What is your answer, Mr. Burgess?" He gave a clear and emphatic statement of his desire to follow Christ, and the whole family was received into the church. From that time on he lived an exemplary Christian life. None of his former companions even invited him to join them in a glass of liquor or in gambling, for they recognized that he had become a new man. He was in his place in church with his family every Sunday morning and evening, and his influence was an inspiration to everyone who knew him. Here was a man who would never have been won if someone had not gone to him personally with the call of Christ. This is the work that wins.

J. O. Peck, a prolific soul winner, said,

If it were revealed to me from heaven by the archangel Gabriel that God had given me the certainty of ten years of life and that, as a condition of my eternal salvation, I must win a thousand souls to Christ in that time, and if it were further conditioned to this end that I might preach every day for the ten years, but might not personally appeal to the unconverted outside the pulpit, or that I might not enter the pulpit during those ten years, but might exclusively appeal to individuals, I would not hesitate one moment to accept the choice of personal effort as the sole means to be used in securing the conversion of ten thousand souls as the condition of my salvation.

Protestant churches particularly have overemphasized the importance of mass appeals through preaching, and have attached too little significance to personal effort in the process of making Christians. It was not so in the New Testament.

84

Under the direction of the Holy Spirit, Philip left a populous city, where he was conducting a revival, to go to a deserted place, evidently because his meeting with a single individual in the mind of the Spirit was even more important to the future of the Kingdom than preaching to crowds of people. If that was the mind of the Spirit in New Testament times, how much more it must be so in our day, when would-be fishers of men standing in their pulpits are often like fishermen casting in a swimming pool where there are no fish. The people they wish to reach are not present in church, yet the nonchurch-going multitudes present a picture of potential wealth for the Kingdom of God.

According to *Everybody's Digest*:

> For six months diamonds worth $243,000 lay untouched in the desert four miles out of Khartoum. They had lain there twinkling in the Sudan sun since the aircraft carrying them had crashed, killing sixteen passengers. Not even hawk-eyed wandering Arabs had seen them up until the time William Charles Crocker came along looking for them.

Crocker dug with his hands in the sands of the desert until he came upon a polished emerald weighing eight carats. Then he found a ruby, and finally diamonds, in the sand. He discovered them only when he searched with keenness and determination, just as we find jewels for the coronet of our King only when we search diligently and personally for them. Like the acres of diamonds Russell H. Conwell used to describe in his lecture by that name, we overlook potential spiritual wealth that lies all around us. Rather let us imitate the woman of whom Jesus told, who, having lost a coin, made minute search for it until she found it. One would suppose everyone attending an evangelistic conference to be a Christian but Lee R. Scarborough, president of the Southwestern Baptist Theological Seminary in Texas, addressing an evangelistic conference in Chicago, made some of us who attended that conference feel that we were not good fishermen when one morning he said: "Last night I asked the little lady who

85

is stenographically reporting this conference if she were a Christian. She replied that she was not. In a brief interview I had the privilege of leading her to Christ. Now, in the South, when one accepts Christ he usually makes some public confession of his new-found faith. I shall therefore ask her if she will come to the platform while we lift our hearts in prayer for her." Touching evidence of this distinguished servant of Christ's sedulousness in searching for souls.

A minister from the Middle West went into a bookstore in Atlanta, Georgia, when the Baptist World Alliance was meeting in that city. He engaged in conversation with the proprietor of the shop. The shopkeeper admitted he was not a Christian, and in a few minutes the minister led him to a decision for Christ. The man invited his visitor to return the next day at the same time. When he arrived at the bookstore he found eight men awaiting him. "Now tell these folks what you told me yesterday," said the proprietor. Six of those men accepted Christ that day in the bookstore. There were fifty thousand Baptists in Atlanta for the convention and here, a stone's throw from the mammoth meetings and in the shadow of great churches, were these unconverted men only waiting for someone to show them the way to Christ.

The pastor of a church near New York was invited by one of his laymen to attend a political banquet in that city. The minister engaged in conversation with the man on his right, who said he was a Presbyterian but had not been in church for seventeen years. The minister asked him to attend a Presbyterian church the next Sunday and then come to his church the following Sunday. The woman on the pastor's left indicated her interest. She said: "I have been the church news reporter of a New York newspaper for fourteen years. I have been in and out of churches during all that time. They have been anxious for me to publish news items about their work, but in all those fourteen years nobody ever has spoken to me about my own spiritual needs." The minister talked briefly with her. Two Sundays later, when he gave the invitation, nine people responded. One of them was the Presbyterian, another the church news reporter.

Personal evangelism reaches not only the initiated but discovers the diamonds and rubies hidden in the sands of worldliness. We frequently make the mistake of going to those whom we judge most likely to respond to Christ's call when the publicans and sinners, drunkards and harlots, whom we overlook, often respond more readily. We attend committee meetings to plan how to rid our communities of liquor without ever trying to reach the people who conduct that nefarious business. A pastor in Camden, New Jersey, had to pass a tavern at the corner of his street every time he came home from his church. His conscience smote him. One day he went in. The people inside knew him. What was this? A pastor—in a tavern? Was he going to order a drink? He walked up to the bar. "I've been wondering about you," he said to the bartender. "Do you ever think of your soul? Christ died to save you." He turned on his heel and walked out. Two Sundays later the tavernkeeper was in the church. At the close of the service he handed the minister a five-dollar bill. "No," said the minister, "we don't want your money. We want your soul." A month later the tavernkeeper accepted Christ and applied for membership in the church.

Personal evangelism not only discovers and wins many people who probably never would be brought to Christ through any other method; it has the advantage of being interpretative. Reference was made earlier in this chapter to Philip winning the Ethiopian eunuch. The eunuch had just come from church. However, he had not received his answer through the services of the church. Nor did he get it from the Bible, which he was reading. In answer to the question "Understandest thou what thou readest?" he said, "How can I, except some man should guide me?" What men often fail to receive through the services of the church and through their own reading of the Bible frequently comes to them through a person who himself knows Christ. The human element is essential in the life-changing process. The transfusion of rich blood comes directly from one life to another as one pours the lifeblood of his faith and redeemed personality into another. There are doubtless many men like the Ethiopian treasurer and the German general, a prisoner of war, who said to an American chaplain: "I know all about military life and tactics. I know how to be a great general and command thousands of men, but I have always been hungry—hungry to know about God." There are thousands of people who are hungry to know about God but who probably never will come to know him without some human guide.

A giant bomber zooming through the frozen North began to sputter. Finally the pilot was compelled to make a forced landing. He found himself in a howling wilderness. For five long days he trudged through the snow in bitter subzero cold to Edmonton, Alberta, seventy-five miles away. All he had to drink was snow water, and all he had to eat was snow. Only faith in God kept him pushing resolutely on his way during those five interminable days. He had not been interested in church. One Sunday he had attended a church in the city in which he was living, out of courtesy to his sister who was visiting him. There he had met some young men who visited him in his boardinghouse until they finally induced him to attend services regularly. When the pilot received his commission in the Army Air Corps the minister invited him to lunch with him in a downtown restaurant. During the meal the pastor asked him if he would be willing to turn his life over to the direction of Christ.

"Is it as simple as that?" he asked incredulously.

"As simple as that," replied the pastor. "There is a great deal of theology I might explain to you, but the simple fact is this—Christ died for you. He offers himself as your Saviour. All you need to do is accept him and turn the direction of your life over to him."

The young lieutenant replied: "If that's what it means, of course I'll do it. I have attended a lot of evangelistic meetings, but they left me confused rather than helped me. No one ever explained the matter to me as you have today."

There in the crowded restaurant the young man had grasped the minister's hand. There had been a word of prayer. Clear as to the meaning of the "great transaction," the young man had publicly confessed Christ and was received into the church before going away to join his unit. During his desolate trek he was drawing upon the faith that had come to him when a man who knew Christ interpreted the gospel to him.

It is not always so easy. People do not always respond readily even to a personal invitation to accept Christ. Often workers are tempted to say, as did a minister in an evangelistic conference: "There is no use. We have visited these people before. They do not wish to unite with us." What would happen to almost any business if its representatives were so easily discouraged? The Presbyterian Minister's Life Insurance Company questioned the advisability of sending the twenty-ninth form letter to prospective policy holders. It was discovered, however, that such good results had come from the twenty-ninth letter that it was decided to continue to send it out. Many people had received twenty-eight letters and had not replied, but many had responded to the twenty-ninth letter. A businessman said: "I made a call once every week for two years on a certain prospective customer before I sold him a single bill of goods, but after I had made more than one hundred calls he began to do business with me and he became my best customer." Can we who are dealing with the eternal destinies of men's souls afford to be less persistent? Too frequently we quit on the borderland of success. One more call might have led to decision and eternal life for some soul.

John Wesley Coates, a sales expert, is fond of telling discouraged salesmen the story of a man who went home one day when it was raining. He saw a kitten on the porch. The kitten had been out in the rain, was very wet, and when the man opened the door it darted into the house. He chased the kitten, caught it, and put it out. A little later the children came home from school, and the kitten got in again. They all had a grand chase and finally caught it and put it out again.

89

After a while the newspaper came. The children heard it hit the front doorstep, and when they went out to get it the kitten got in for the third time. While the children were chasing the kitten and putting it out once more, the man was down in the basement looking around. It was nice and warm down there and he saw a box standing in one corner. He thought to himself: "We probably need a cat. I'll just get some old rags and put them in the box and the next time the kitten gets in I'll bring it down in the basement and give it a home." The kitten didn't return. After dinner the man walked around the yard looking for it, but it didn't show up. If that kitten had made just one more call it would have won a home for life!

Gipsy Smith used to tell of an experience he had in John Henry Jowett's church in England when he went there to preach. Jowett announced to his congregation: "Joe won his man for Christ." Then turning to where the man sat, he asked: "Joe, how many times did you go after him?" A rather shabbily dressed man stood to his feet. He was probably an ordinary workingman. A broad smile diffused itself over his weather-beaten countenance. "I went after him seventy-nine times, but the eightieth time he came to church and accepted Christ." His smile became yet more radiant as he concluded: "And he's here with me now." Evidently he considered going after one man eighty times worth all the time and effort entailed. Here was a workingman, a prince flushed with victory, "his jewel in his hand." We naturally desire immediacy, but the dividends on our investment of time and effort do not always come at once. Evangelistic effort is often a long-range investment.

In Maine two women called upon a family to invite them to accept Christ and unite with their little church. They came away disappointed because there was no immediate response, but they asked several people to join them in prayer for the family. Two months passed and nothing happened. One day the pastor's phone rang. A voice at the other end inquired: "When could we unite with the church?" "Come forward in response to the invitation on Sunday morning," the pastor

90

suggested. They did. It was the couple upon whom the two women had called two months before who came forward the next Sunday morning. But they did not come alone. In addition to the two there came the woman's unmarried sister, another sister and her husband, and the husband's brother, together with the mother and father of the three women. A visit that seemed a failure resulted in the decisions of eight people. Not all at once, but drop by drop blood comes into the anemic persons who are about to perish, but it means rich abundant life—eternal life. Many persons have been willing to give their blood to blood banks during the war. Every minister ought to strive to make his members realize that transfusing the blood of their Christ-indwelt personalities is the most important and rewarding work in the world. His responsibility is not discharged when he himself engages in this work to which his Master gave himself unceasingly. Jesus also trained his disciples to go in quest of individuals and fired them with enthusiasm for the task.

When people saw the converts constantly coming into Lyman Beecher's church in Boston, they asked: "How do you do so much?" "I do not do it," the learned pastor replied. "I preach on the Sabbath as hard as I can, and I have four hundred church members who go out and preach every day in the week. They are preaching all the time, and that is the way, with God's blessing, we get along so well." Beecher had trained his people just as a minister in Louisville, Kentucky, in more recent years, trained his people. He conducted a training class for church officers in his study every Sunday morning. In that church every officer and every Sunday-school teacher had to agree that he would make it his supreme business and use his office in the church to win people to Christ. Anyone who was unwilling to enter into that agreement could not hold office. Of course that pastor built a great church. During the ten years of his pastorate he stated that there were only three Sundays when there was no response to the public invitation to accept Christ and unite with the church. Another minister attributes the remarkable growth of his

91

church to two things: the organization of personal workers and the giving of the invitation at *every* service. He says: "Our personal workers alone have brought more than seven hundred members into the fellowship of this church; and they, plus the invitation, brought five last Sunday, six the Sunday before, eight others for baptism last Sunday night, and so on—new people practically every Sunday for six years, which is a thrilling experience for both pastor and people. Frankly I wouldn't know how to build a church without these two means, yet many pastors apparently do not know of such aids to evangelism and many more have never used them! If we really want a great ingathering I don't know how we can do otherwise."

The pastor of a church of sixty members developed a prospect list of twelve hundred. His people spent one evening each week for two years in visitation. The church now has a membership of 240 and is adding about one hundred members each year. We can reach the mass only through the man. Every church should have a representative evangelistic committee. When the responsibility is left with the officials of the church it is difficult to stimulate the enthusiasm of all the people; but when leaders of men, women, and young people, as well as the officers and teachers of the Sunday school, are brought into the planning and work, they may all be enlisted and saved from rusting in inexcusable idleness.

A speaker in a ministers' conference told of coming down a mountain in California and watching something that sparkled and flashed brilliantly in the sun. It could not be a lake; in fact he could not imagine what it could be until his descent was completed. Then the mystery was solved. What he had seen from the heights was a field of thousands of glittering airplanes standing wing to wing. He paused to ask some questions of a man along the road. The man said: "Yes, they represent an awful cost, and if they stand here six months longer they'll be useless. Not a one of them will ever be able to fly again." The fascinating picture suddenly turned dark —potential power becoming junk.

There is, however, a sadder disillusionment than that. It is a church which, when viewed from a distance, appears great, a large congregation, an eloquent preacher, and plenty of money, but on closer scrutiny one realizes that there are people who have been bought at awful cost and who might rise to great heights and accomplish marvelous things for God, but who remain idle, their potential power ebbing away in inactivity—inactivity that inevitably becomes corrosive until it renders God's people useless.

VIII

The Shadow of a Rock

As soon as they had secured a modest home in which to begin their life together, a young couple, married in Chicago, did the next most important thing for any couple to do. They searched for a church home. Although neither of them was a Baptist, they seemed to feel most at home in a certain inconspicuous Baptist church of some one hundred and fifty members. No one asked them to join the church. They themselves sought out the minister and said: "We should like to be immersed and unite with this church." He seemed very much surprised but nonetheless he began clearing the old clothing and shoes out of the long-dry baptismal pool where they had been stored.

The pastor of that church was not evangelistic in method. The new member asked him one Sunday: "How is it you never give people a chance to accept Christ in this church?"

Somewhat taken back, the minister asked: "What do you mean?"

"Why don't you give an invitation at the close of the services?"

The pastor thought no one would be likely to respond.

"On the contrary," said the young layman, "I have been talking to a man about Christ, and I have some reason to believe he would come forward and declare himself if he were given a chance."

The minister yielded to his new member's suggestion. The next Sunday he invited anyone who wished to accept Christ to come forward. The young man mentioned to the pastor promptly responded. That was the beginning of the influence in that church of the young layman James L. Kraft, later president of the Kraft-Phenix Cheese Corporation—and the

94

beginning of the growth of that inconspicuous little Baptist church into the influential North Shore Church of Chicago, now numbering some 2,500 members, a large membership for a Northern Baptist church.

In time Kraft became superintendent of the Sunday school, which often has over a thousand in attendance. He will travel any number of miles in order to be in his place in church and Sunday school each Sunday. Such can be the influence of a consecrated layman who is determined to see the work of Christ go forward.

The history of Tremont Temple, New England's largest Protestant church, which Dwight L. Moody called the greatest preaching station in the world, is largely the story of strong, consecrated laymen who lived to exalt Christ and make their church great. Their success in business was doubtless due in some measure at least to the fact that early in life they heeded the call "seek ye first the kingdom of God." There was a glorious succession of men like Timothy Gilbert, who, because of racial prejudice in other churches at the time, bought the Tremont Theater and there organized a new church in which there would be no distinction of color, class, or creed. George W. Chipman soon joined Timothy Gilbert and saved the building by paying the mortage. He became foremost in Christian service, a mighty hunter before the Lord, who introduced Russell H. Conwell to Jesus Christ, an account of which I shall give later in this volume. One day at church he met a boy by the name of Leonard Rhodes. "You're going home to dinner with me," he told the lad who still had hayseed in his hair. Leonard and his brother Edgar had left the farm where they had grown up in poverty. When they left, their folks said: "You're going to a big city. We can't give you anything more than five dollars, but we are giving you a precious book. Read it and live by its teachings. Find a church and attend it." They became members of Tremont Temple.

One day Leonard came to Deacon Chipman and said: "I'd like to go into business."

"That's fine," the deacon replied; "what's stopping you?"

"I haven't any money."

"I'll fix that up," the deacon assured him.

The Rhodes brothers worked hard. Up at five in the morning to get to Fanuel Hall market and select produce to be sold in their store, they would be at the store in time for it to open. But they lived for their Lord and Tremont Temple. Leonard spent his evenings quietly with his wife, and about nine-thirty he would say: "Now, my dear, we have had a pleasant evening. I've had a long busy day but I must leave you now because I must do at least two hours work for my church." He and his brother never missed a meeting at Tremont Temple. He would leave a house full of company to be in his place. They poured their wealth into the church and they devoted all their manly energies to the development of the great work there.

A boy in Los Angeles was pronounced dead by doctors, but two firemen with an inhalator worked over him for more than an hour and restored the revived child to his mother. Even a church considered dead by doctors of divinity may be revived and restored to its Lord by determined laymen. The scriptures say: "A man shall be . . . as the shadow of a great rock in a weary land." Who can measure the influence or appraise the possibilities of a single strong man standing like a citadel. He can not only bring to pass the seemingly impossible, but by his influence attract other men of ability to his church. Men rally to the leadership of other successful and energetic Christian laymen. They also set a standard of excellence in church procedure. Their painstaking work shames and often transforms those who might otherwise do shoddy work for the Lord and his church. Laymen are usually the power behind great churches and great movements. At a meeting of the Episcopal Club of Boston, Dean George Hodges, of the Episcopal Divinity School, once spoke of the leadership of laymen in historic religious awakenings: "There have been three notable periods in the history of the extension of the Christian religion," he said, "the time of the martyrs, the time of the monks, and the time of the Methodists. In each of these periods religion spread phenomenally. The significance of each

96

of these for our present purpose is that each of them was an era of lay activity. The Christian Church was begun by laymen; the apostles were all laymen. It has ever since owed its best growth to the co-operation of laymen. The monks were lay orders. The Methodists won their great victories by lay preaching. Not only that, but these laymen in every one of these three periods did their work in spite of the clergy, discouraged by the clergy, detested by the clergy."

We may be thankful that in our day there are few ministers who would consciously discourage their laymen, but there are many ministers who have small appreciation of the limitless potential in their laymen, and there are some defeated and discouraged ministers who might become successful if they were given the encouragement and wholehearted support of strong laymen, laymen who now seem disinterested, leaving the pastor to carry the whole load of parish responsibility.

On the other hand it has been said that in many places laymen are more eager for evangelism than ministers. After all, the Old Testament prophets were laymen, farmers called to service from between the handles of the plow, gatherers of sycamore fruit, cupbearers to kings. The New Testament apostles were also laymen recruited from the receipt of custom and fishermen's boats. The apostolate of the laity must be restored, for laymen can build great churches and great preachers.

When someone remarked on the long line of successful pastors who had served a certain church, one of the laymen of that church said: "We won't let a minister fail in our church." A member of John Henry Jowett's great church in New York visited the little chapel in England which Jowett had once served. He thanked one of the men of the chapel for the man of God they had sent to the United States. "Give us ten years more," replied the layman, "and we'll give you another great man of God. This church makes great men of God."

Laymen are responsible for the work of the pulpit, for a preacher cannot long do a work in which his men have no heart and to which they refuse to give their support. The laymen are the continuing and integrating force in our churches.

Ministers come and go—it is reported that in a Western state there is a 50 per cent turnover of pastors in one denomination every year—but the laymen generally remain in the churches. Because they are the continuing element in the work, to a great extent they determine the character and complexion of the work. If the laymen are unspiritual, in all probability the church will be unspiritual. If the laymen care for the souls of men and seek them, the church will be evangelistic. No pastor can remain indifferent to a movement in which his laymen take an active part. Laymen are not particularly interested in the theological contests that so frequently limit the influence of their ministers and hold back the work of God's Kingdom.

Charles L. Goodell once asked a New York millionaire, who had in his younger days been active in the church: "Why are you less zealous than formerly? Have you become skeptical as to the truths you once held?" Almost savagely the millionaire replied: "I am weary with the constant attention which the ministers pay to skepticism. I am a member of many clubs and I meet on intimate terms many of the wealthy and influential men of New York. I know how they feel concerning religion and the church. At heart they are orthodox. They believe in the great verities—God, sin, salvation, immortality. They do not care to sit through a discussion of the latest phase of German rationalism or English agnosticism. They feel the need of the appeal to conscience which they heard as boys and which has so largely disappeared from many pulpits. We know our duty, we need to be stirred up to do it."

Laymen want action and there is crying need for their action today. American youth adrift, in desperate need of faith. Let the laymen provide them positive leadership. Many of our best men should consider serving as superintendents or teachers in Sunday schools. Democracy's only defense against atheistic communism is Christianity. Communistic cells in our colleges are tirelessly at work to destroy this defense. Successful businessmen are needed to speak publicly and counsel young people privately on Christian principles and the need of enlisting for Christ.

In *The Sun Is Up* Franklin D. Elmer tells of a commonplace but significant happening. Sitting on the side of a mountain he saw a milkweed seed borne on the breeze from the valley below floating upward above his head. He knew that somewhere on the mountain there would be another milkweed plant because a plant was sending out its seed to produce new plants. That is the nature of living things. Jesus said that the children of the Kingdom are seed. The world will never be saved by ordained ministers or formal missionaries. There are not enough of them. In New Testament times Jewish-Christian laymen proved themselves seed. As informal missionaries they carried the gospel to Phoenicia, far to the north, between the Lebanon range and the sea, and Cyprus, a large island more than sixty miles west of Palestine, and Antioch in northern Syria. They could not hold their peace, for their hearts overflowed with the glad tidings. Jesus had prayed not only for his followers but also "for them also who shall believe on me through their word."

I was sitting on the porch of a cottage in Maine one summer when a huckster stopped in front.

"Vant any corn or beets this morning?" he inquired.

I replied: "No, we do not want anything. We have been to town and made our purchases."

"I have got the nicest celery you ever saw."

We did not want any celery.

"I have a fine hand of bananas for twenty-five cents. Better than you can buy in Boston for thirty cents."

I said: "No, we don't want anything this morning, but you are a good salesman."

The huckster looked up appreciatively and with a shrug said: "Vell, if I vouldn't talk you vouldn't know vat I got."

No man will know what we have in Christianity unless informal missionaries "tell the story of Jesus and his love." Laymen can be salesmen for God. Many of them are agents or salesmen in the business world. They are trained to meet people and influence them commercially. They can influence people for Christ. This is as much their business as working

99

for some commercial organization is their business. Uncle John Vassar was well known in the part of the country where I grew up. He was a tireless personal worker. One day he talked with a woman in a Boston hotel lobby. When he left there were tears in the woman's eyes. When her husband returned he inquired as to what had upset her. She told him of the strange little man and of what he had said. Her husband asked: "Why didn't you tell him to mind his own business?"

"Dear," she replied, "if you had been here you would have thought it was his business."

Reuben A. Torrey once said: "I would like to ask what right any man has to call himself a follower of Jesus Christ if he is not a soul winner? There is absolutely no such thing as following Christ unless you can make the purpose of Christ's life the purpose of your life." Winning men is the Christian's business although he may not use John Vassar's method. Let each man do it in his own way. Let us use our friendships and personal influence for Christ. A survey was made on "What Iowans Think of Religion." According to its findings only 6 per cent of church members joined the church because of doctrinal belief; 67 per cent joined because of the influence of relatives or friends who were members of the church. Some laymen are in labor organizations; some, by virtue of the fact that they are employers, deal with men in the labor organizations. They have an opportunity, greater than that of any pastor, to influence men for Christ.

During World War II, I addressed the chaplains and civilian ministers at Camp McCoy, Wisconsin, on personal witnessing for Christ. Colonel Ewert came to me at the close of the address and told me that his father was a Methodist minister, stationed for a number of years at Matoon, Illinois. He said: "My father was always out on the streets visiting people, and as a result he almost never had a service without someone responding to the invitation to accept Christ. But the evangelistic results in that church were not due entirely to my father. There was a man by the name of Collins in the congregation. Collins ran a men's furnishing store. He never lost an opportunity to introduce men to Christ. Being a good salesman he knew the approach should be natural, friendly, and informal, and he'd say to a man, after he had fitted a suit to him, 'That suit will look well on you in church next Sunday,' or when he had sold a tie he'd say to the purchaser, 'That's a nice tie; it will look well on you. I suppose you'll sport that tie at church next Sunday.' That was a diplomatic and friendly approach and opened the way to talk about the church and Christ, and many a man was won for Christ and the church there in Collins' Haberdashery."

In his *Life of St. Francis of Assisi* Paul Sabatier says:

It is not easy to hear and apply to one's self the exhortations of preachers who, aloft in the pulpit, seem to be carrying out a mere formality; it is just as difficult to escape from the appeals of a layman who walks at our side. The amazing multitude of Protestant sects is due in a great degree to this superiority of lay preaching over clerical. The most brilliant orators of the Christian pulpits are bad converters; their eloquent appeals may captivate the imagination and lead a few men of the world to the foot of the altar, but these results are not more brilliant than ephemeral. But let a peasant or a workingman speak to those whom he meets, a few simple words going directly to the conscience, and the man is always impressed, often won.[1]

A director of evangelism in a Western state went with a humble engineer to visit another engineer. The director talked at length and seemed to be making no impression upon the prospect. The other visitor had remained quiet. Suddenly he said: "Jim, there ain't nothin' like it." That simple statement turned the tide. What the trained worker with all his skill could not do, that simple statement of his unlearned companion accomplished and won their man.

In his book *New Testament Evangelism* Arthur C. Archibald says:

A man in Kansas who had been a commonplace Christian heard the author say: "No Christian ought to be comfortable so long as

[1] By permission of Charles Scribner's Sons.

a single unsaved man remains in his community." He pondered it. It made him uncomfortable. He took the matter to God. There was born in his soul a great conviction. He began to speak to his casual acquaintances about spiritual things. He was surprised at the response shown. His power of presentation grew. Little by little he was able to lead men into a definite decision.

On the day I left that city he took me aside and said: "Pastor, I want to show you something before you leave us." "Well," I said, "what is it?"

"Just this," he said. And he took from his pocket a little notebook that seemed to be filled with names. "In this book" he said, "you will find listed the names of 122 men whom I have been the means of leading to Christ these past two years. Two years ago, as you know, God gave me an awful shaking up. From that day, as I have been on my trips, I have been doing business for him. I used to be very content to do nothing. Now I am uncomfortable when I am not working for him." [2]

In New Testament times the laymen who brought the gospel as far as Antioch made the mistake of telling the story of Jesus to the wrong people. They didn't think of the gospel as belonging to some certain coterie. They didn't know any better than to communicate the gospel to the despised Gentiles, and so they blundered into nameless immortality. Philip had a great mission in Samaria; Peter began a great work with Cornelius, but nothing much seemed to come directly out of either promising effort, yet these unknown Jews planted seed that grew and grew into a plant entirely different in form and extent from anything anyone had anticipated. Untrained laymen need not fear making mistakes. God can take mistakes and make marvels of them. Antioch became the center of the greatest movement of Christianity, the hub from which Christianity moved out in widening circles of influence, influence felt in all parts of the world. Christian laymen must win all kinds of people in today's world, rich and poor, learned and ignorant, employer and employee, capitalist and laborer. They must see worth in the disinherited and potential beauty in the unlovely.

In a National Academy of Design competition a prize of $500 was awarded a picture entitled "Jersey Junk." It represented one of those repulsive graveyards of outworn jalopies that blot the landscape of almost every town. Yet an artist had enough insight to discover in it sufficient beauty and significance to make it worthy of his effort, and the judges had recognized in it merit enough to justify an award. It requires a measure of greatness as well as love to discern the spiritual possibilities in an outcast person of a mongrel race met amid the commonplace contacts of a public well, as our Lord saw them.

A missionary visiting a little crippled boy in a garret in a poor quarter of London saw an orange on the bed.

"Where did you get the orange?" he asked.

"A man brought it to me," the boy replied. "A man who often comes and reads the Bible to me and prays with me and brings me good things to eat."

The missionary asked the visitor's name.

"I forget his name," the lad said, "but he makes speeches in that great building."

"The Houses of Parliament?"

"Yes, that's it, the Houses of Parliament."

"Could his name be Gladstone?" the missionary inquired.

"Yes, Mr. Gladstone, that's his name," the boy beamed.

William E. Gladstone, perhaps the greatest statesman England ever produced, was big enough, like his Master, to include visitations to an obscure sick child among the many demands made upon his crowded schedule.

A top executive of a large corporation was teamed up with a humble businessman in a visitation campaign in a church. The humble member of the team said: "Because of his financial and social position he could easily have snubbed me but instead he seemed glad to go with me." Most of the assignments had been made by the time the two men received their cards. The addresses on them were not on the best streets in town;

103

in fact they indicated that they were boardinghouses on the fringe of the slums. The big executive said: "Let us take these cards; probably nobody else will want them." As his expensive car drew up before a dilapidated dwelling he laid his hand on his companion's arm and said: "Just a moment. This is a serious undertaking. Let us go to the throne of grace for guidance." After a brief prayer they knocked on a door in the dark, dingy hallway. The disheveled man who answered the knock appeared furtive. The executive said: "We have come to talk to you about spiritual things. Is it well with your soul?" The man broke down and said: "No, it is not; the police are after me. When you knocked I was afraid it was they." The man clung to his two visitors as a drowning man would grasp at anything which might offer promise of saving him. The important executive did not begrudge the hour spent in leading the poor soul to Christ. The more humble member of the team said: "From that night on I have been glad to take the undesirable assignments because of my realization of the needs of men." One can never tell what the results of winning such humble people may be.

On his journeys Bishop Asbury crossed a bridge on which he saw a colored man. He was the blackest man he had ever seen. An inner voice urged the bishop to speak to this man about Christ. He asked him his name. He replied: "Punch."

"No, I don't want to know your nickname; what is your real name?" insisted the bishop.

"Punch. That's all the name I have," replied the Negro.

There on the bridge the bishop led the man to Christ. Years afterward an old colored man appeared at the door of Bishop Asbury's home. When the bishop greeted him he asked: "Do you remember me?"

"No," said the bishop.

He said: "I'm Punch."

Then Bishop Asbury remembered the conversation on the bridge long years before. The colored man said: "I've come to ask you to send a preacher to my people. I'm old; I'm not going to live very long, and they need a preacher."

When the bishop questioned the colored man, he told him he had talked to his people about Christ and some of them 'had become Christians and needed a preacher to shepherd them.

The bishop asked: "How many Christians are there?"

"I got about three hundred," replied Punch.

In a town in Nebraska the people kept saying to the evangelist who was conducting meetings: "There is a man here who is good for a hundred men for Christ if you can get him."

"Who is he?"

"John Champney, the miller."

When the minister went to him, he listened, went to the cupboard, took out a flask of whisky, and smashed it on the stones. With tears rolling down his cheeks he said: "People have pointed their fingers at me and called me an old drunkard but you are the first man who has ever asked me to be a Christian." At last he was persuaded to go to the church, and in less than a week after his conversion seventy-eight followed him.

We must also win men of influence—leaders of men. In his *Autobiography* Charles G. Finney tells the story of a certain judge in Rochester, New York. He held a high place in the estimation of his profession. Finney says:

As Judge G——'s wife was a particular friend of mine, I had occasion to see him not unfrequently, and was very sure that the Word was getting a strong hold of him. I was going on from night to night but had not thought my somewhat new and select audience yet prepared for me to call for any decision on the part of inquirers. But I had arrived at a point where I thought it was time to draw the net ashore. I had been carefully laying it around the whole mass of lawyers hedging them in, as I supposed, by a train of reasoning that they could not resist. I was aware that lawyers are accustomed to listen to argument, to feel the weight of a logically presented truth; and had no doubt that the great majority of them were thoroughly convinced, as far as I had gone; consequently I had prepared a discourse which I intended should bring them to the point, and if it appeared to take effect I intended to call on them to commit themselves. Judge G——, at the time I was there

105

before, when his wife was converted, had opposed the anxious seat. I expected he would do so again, as I knew he had strongly committed himself, in what he said, against the use of the anxious seat. When I came to preach the sermon of which I have spoken I observed that Judge G—— was not in the seat he had usually occupied; and on looking around I could not see him anywhere among the members of the bar or the judges. I felt concerned about this, for I had prepared myself with reference to his case. I knew his influence was great, and that if he would take a decided stand it would have a very great influence upon all the legal profession in the city. However, I soon observed that he had come into the gallery and had found a seat just at the head of the gallery stairs, where he sat wrapped in his cloak. I went on with my discourse; but near the close of what I designed to say, I observed that Judge G—— had gone from his seat. I felt distressed, for I concluded that, as it was cold where he sat and perhaps there was some confusion, it being near the head of the stairs, he had gone home; and hence that the sermon, which I had prepared with my eye upon him, had failed to take its effect.

From the basement room of the church there was a narrow stairway into the audience-room above, coming up just by the side of, and partly behind, the pulpit. Just as I was drawing my sermon to a close and with my heart almost sinking with the fear that I was going to fail in what I had hoped to secure that night, I felt someone pulling at the skirt of my coat. I looked around, and there was Judge G——. He had gone down through the basement room and up those narrow stairs and crept up the pulpit steps far enough to reach me and pull me by the coat. When I turned around to him, and beheld him with great surprise, he said to me: "Mr. Finney, won't you pray for me by name and I will take the anxious seat?"

As he came up on the pulpit stairs, and when I announced to them what he said, it produced a wonderful shock. There was a great gush of feeling in every part of the house. Many held down their heads and wept; others seemed to be engaged in earnest prayer. He crowded around in front of the pulpit and immediately knelt down. The lawyers arose almost en masse and crowded into the aisles and filled the open space in front, wherever they could get a place to kneel. The movement had begun without my requesting it; but then I publicly invited any who were prepared to renounce their sins and give their hearts to God and to accept

106

Christ and His salvation, to come forward, into the aisles, or wherever they could, and kneel down. There was a mighty movement.[8]

There is always a mighty movement when leaders are won. By winning the leaders of thought in the United States laymen can start a mighty national movement back to a forsaken God, back to Christ, the Bible, the church, and to Christian living. Even though it seems impossible for ministers, because they are looked upon as an official class, laymen can do it. The future of the Kingdom depends largely upon them, as it did in New Testament times, and as it has since the Reformation returned the church to the congregation. The mightiest movements in Kingdom advance have been lay movements. The next great advance in Protestant Christianity waits upon the laymen. The salvation of many a local church can come only through a consecrated and determined laity.

* By permission of Fleming H. Revell Co.

IX

Hearthstones

MARGARET SLATTERY ONCE TOLD of a young girl brought in from a swimming accident apparently dead. She said: "We the helpless, useless crowd stood there. We could do nothing. We knew neither what nor how. Suddenly the crowd parted at the command of a young woman who had been rushed to the scene in an automobile. She was a trained nurse. Calm, quiet, determined, she knew just what to do and did it. In twenty minutes the physician came and in a few moments the girl breathed once, then again and again, and once more she lived. The physician shook the nurse's hand and said, 'You saved her.' " Said Miss Slattery: "I could not get over the marvel of it as a few days later I saw that girl alive, walking about, restored to all who loved her because someone 'knew how.' " And she said that as she thought of this friend and that one out of Christ, and of this young man and that one who used to be in Sunday school but now stood on the street smoking cigarettes, she determined to make an earnest effort to "know how."

The good women of America need not stand by helplessly watching their country sink to lower levels, their children and their neighbor's children go from bad to worse, their friends attempting to live without God and without hope in the world. They may learn how to reach them for Christ. O. P. Gifford once insisted in his morning sermon that it is the duty of every Christian constantly to be winning souls. "Every Christian can win somebody to Christ," he insisted. At the close of the service a woman said to him: "This is the first time I have heard you when you seemed unfair; you repeatedly said that every Christian could win somebody to Christ. You made no exceptions. I am an exception. I work

108

every day early and late; I have no education and no opportunity."

Gifford asked: "Does no one ever come to your house? Does the milkman never come, nor the grocer? What about the bread man?"

The next day when the milkman came to the house, after a battle with herself, the woman overcame her reluctance and fear. She said: "Wait a minute. I have a question to ask you. Are you a Christian?"

The man looked at her in amazement. "What made you ask that?" he questioned. "For two nights I have not been able to sleep for thinking about that matter. I do want to be a Christian."

That humble woman who said she had no opportunity and no education showed the man how to accept Christ, and before a year had elapsed she had won seven persons to Christ and into church membership. In this work "knowing how" is largely a matter of "wanting to." Izaak Walton laughed at the idea that you can teach the art of catching fish through a book, for "that art," he insists, "is not to be taught by words." There is a precious Book that helps greatly in the art of winning persons for Christ's Kingdom, but love and a sense of the desperate needs of people will always find a way.

Never was there a time in modern life when the interests of women, and the things upon which women depend for safety and happiness, have been so endangered. The Christian women of the United States must arise to the challenge of a spiritual awakening. Their field of service is different from that of the men but it is no less essential, and it lies nearer their own interests. The increase in divorce is alarming. There is today one divorce for every three marriages. In numbers of communities there are as many divorces as there are marriages. The country is threatened with a return to the morality of the barnyard. This strikes at the foundations of life. As goes the home, so goes the nation. Probably no more gripping evidence of the influence of the home for good or ill has ever been given than by the comparison which has been made between the Jukes family and the Edwards family. There was no spiritual life in the Jukes home. There were approximately 1,200 persons in the five succeeding generations after Jukes. Of them none was even moderately educated. Only 20 of them learned a trade, and 10 of these learned theirs in a state prison. There were 310 professional paupers who were kept in the poorhouse an aggregate of 2,300 years. There were nearly 50 of the women who were notoriously immoral. At least 400 of the men and women were physically wrecked because of wickedness. There were 7 murderers, 60 habitual thieves, and 130 others who were convicted of various other crimes.

Jonathan Edwards and his wife, on the other hand, built their home on Christ. Among the five generations of his descendants there were 285 college graduates among the men alone. There were 30 college presidents and 65 others who were college professors. Many others were ministers, principals of academies, professional men, and mothers of happy families.

In the chapel of an Indian mission at Lodge Grass, Montana, there is a window picturing a tepee and a cross. It was given to the chapel by a man who said: "I want this picture to bear the message to everyone who looks at it that only the Man of the cross can save the people who live in tepees." We may go a step further and say only the Man of the cross can save those who live in homes, and save the homes in which they live.

A young lawyer in Detroit said: "I have to handle many divorce cases—three new ones this week. I belong to a church of fifteen hundred members but I have had to handle only one divorce case for members of that church. Christ's people do not go to the divorce court." Evangelism, through which people are won to Christ and his way of life, is the safeguard of marriage and the home. Christ has the solution for the problems of the home. He can make marriage successful and permanent. The fruits of his spirit—love, joy, peace, longsuffering, meekness, temperance, gentleness, goodness, faith—are the elements upon which happiness in marriage depends.

When the United States returns to Christ it will return to happy homes, warmed by marital love and cheered by normal children, secure in the sense of parental affection, growing up in the love of God into Christian manhood and womanhood. In my boyhood I heard a story of a lighthouse keeper whose son ran away to sea. As the father lighted his lamp each evening when darkness came on he thought of his sailor lad and prayed for his safety. But years passed and the boy did not return. The father grew careless about his tasks. He did not always clean his lamp; sometimes he was late in filling and lighting it. Then one night he forgot to light it. A terrific storm came on, and when the lighthouse keeper awoke in the morning he saw a wrecked ship at the foot of the cliff. The light of day revealed dead bodies on the shore. He went to examine them and to his horror he recognized among them his own son, come back at last, but dead through his own father's neglect to keep his light burning. Parents have a great deal to answer for in the moral failure of their children and the moral degeneracy of their day.

At a conference on delinquency prevention held in Chicago, a boy 15 years of age said: "If a child knows that he will have fun by getting to know his parents better, he will stay home. But if, when he is home, they aren't or they just read the paper, he will go out and stir up some excitement for himself."

A girl of the same age said she did not think adults realize "how much children want the companionship of their parents." What greater evangelistic opportunity is offered Christian parents than that which comes through fellowship with their children?

Enemies of the home are multiplying among us. The divorce rate has increased from a ratio of one divorce to every six marriages before World War II to one divorce to every three marriages since the war. Before the war 6 per cent of American women smoked; now 67 per cent smoke. And we have arrived at an all-time high in liquor consumption largely because of the vast number of women now drinking. The magazines glamorize liquor as part of the vast propaganda of the liquor forces, and it is said that wherever there is propaganda there is always a proper goose to swallow it.

A Washington policewoman reported: "We find children hunting their parents who are so busy getting drunk that they have no time to stay at home. Two of my women saw a couple of nice little kids at eleven o'clock at night outside a tavern. They said: 'Mother and Dad are in there and they won't come out.'" Half of the boys and girls that go wrong, half of the infidels of our land, would be law-abiding citizens and lovers of God if they had been nurtured in truly Christian homes. Henry W. Grady, editor of the *Atlanta Constitution*, sought to restore to the South her lost heritage during the days following the Civil War. In his book *Helping Others to Become Christians* Roland Q. Leavell says of Grady:

He went to legislative halls, hoping that wise legislation would rebuild a Christian society. Despairing there, he went to the schools, saying that if young people were taught to think right, they would live right. Later he said that the Sunday schools were more helpful than the schools, for spiritual hearts are more effective even than clear minds. Eventually Mr. Grady found the true hope of the land when he spent the night in a humble log cabin in the piney woods of his state. He sat before the open fireside until bedtime, talking about the affairs of the outside world. Before retiring, the father asked Mr. Grady to join them in their family devotions. The mother took the large family Bible, opened its pages toward the light from the crackling pine knots on the hearth, and read aloud from the Word of God. Then the family knelt while the father prayed. He called his sons by name, asking God to make them good citizens of the land and of the kingdom of heaven. He prayed for his two daughters, asking God to keep them pure and modest and holy. Mr. Grady said that there he found the greatest hope for the future of the land.[1]

There is indeed the greatest field of opportunity for serving the future of the land, but what parents do they must do

[1] By permission of the Home Mission Board, Southern Baptist Convention, Atlanta.

promptly. The days of childhood pass all too quickly, and Yale psychologists, who have given careful study to the matter, say that more can be done for the religious life before a baby is eighteen months old than can be done after that.

In his book *Evangelism in Christian Education* Richard L. Ownbey maintains that children usually become Christians in a good home very much as boys become farmers. Born and reared on a farm and taught by a farmer-father to love farm life, it is natural that a boy should think in terms of agriculture for a vocation. And I should like to add the perfect naturalness of the process of selection is likely to make him a better and not worse farmer than the one who comes into agriculture over a totally different avenue. By the same token, children born in a Christian home and brought up in an atmosphere of devotion and Christian living by earnest Christian parents are likely to become Christians, not through a cataclysmic conversion but in a quiet, natural commitment of their lives to their mother's and father's Christ.

Herself the twenty-fifth child of her parents, Susanna Wesley was married at nineteen and bore her husband nineteen children in twenty-one years, of whom John Wesley was the fifteenth. Bringing up her family on a wage which a modern mechanic would despise, she not only provided for their material needs but for their spiritual lives as well. In one of her letters she tells how deeply impressed she was on reading the story of the evangelistic efforts of Danish missionaries in India. "It came into my mind," she says, "that I might do more than I do. I resolved to begin with my own children. I take such proportion of time as I can best spare to discourse every night with each child by itself." Later on people began to marvel at her remarkable influence over her children. "There is no mystery about the matter," she writes again. "I just took Molly alone with me into my own room every Monday night, Hetty every Tuesday night, Nancy every Wednesday night, Jacky every Thursday night, and so on, all through the week; that was all!" Her reward was the confidence of her children. "I cannot remember," says John Wesley, "I cannot remember ever having kept back a doubt from my mother; she was the one heart to whom I went in absolute confidence, from my babyhood until the day of her death." A generation of mothers like Susanna Wesley would bring about a world revival. Indeed someone says: "The history of revivals is the story of praying mothers." Parents promote the Kingdom through their children when they are alive to their spiritual opportunities. At Dwight L. Moody's funeral at Northfield, W. R. Moody, the elder son, standing amid the bereaved members of the Moody family in the front seat in the church, asked the presiding officer if he might say a word. He told of his father's dealings with him and his brother and sister. Then in closing he gave utterance to the following testimony: "Dwight L. Moody won each of his own children to Jesus Christ."

Christian women are responsible not only for their own children and their own homes but for other children and other homes. A humble Christian woman met a little boy on the street in Louisville, Kentucky. She asked him if he attended Sunday school. He replied in the negative. She promised to stop for him and take him to Sunday school with her the next Sunday if he would be ready. Discovering that he had no parents, she took him into her home and sent him to school, then to high school and college. Under her influence he decided to prepare for the ministry. One day before he graduated from theological seminary she asked him to consider the foreign field. Harry Meyers went to Japan. One day there was a knock at the door. Meyers found a tearful little Japanese boy on the porch. Through his tears he asked: "Is it true that Jesus Christ died for men because he loved them?" The missionary led the little lad—Toyohiko Kagawa—to a decision for Christ. When one realizes the immense influence for the Kingdom of God exercised by Kagawa, the revivals he has inaugurated, and the new movement for three million new converts in Japan which he has recently launched, one begins to understand something of the vast influence for Christ women may exert.

The women's society in most of our churches can enter into greater areas of usefulness in the deepening of the spiritual life of its members, the winning of new members to Christian discipleship and service, the reclamation of those who have become indifferent or discouraged. The women's society can help to train parents in ways of leading their children to definite and intelligent decision for Christ. It can help parents to understand the cruciality of infancy in future Christian living, the child's religious ideas, how Christian character is developed, how to have a home whose atmosphere will be a spiritual asset rather than a liability, how to develop a child's loyalty to Christ and the church, how to meet moral crises in childhood and youth, and form a program which would enlist parents as the greatest force in an ongoing evangelistic program in our churches.

Women are most effective in visitation evangelism. The more education and training in knowing how, the better; but they do not need education or much training to be successful.

A missionary from Lodge Grass Indian Mission in Montana tells of a visitation campaign conducted by the mission. One of the Indian women didn't appear the first night for visitation. The missionary went to her and asked why she hadn't come. She said: "I thought I wouldn't be missed." The missionary replied: "You're part of this plan. You're missed just as much as one of the screws or springs would be missed if it dropped out of my watch. Your partner is waiting to go with you." She took the two to a home and waited in the car while they made their visit. They went reluctantly, scarcely knowing how to begin, but they had no sooner gotten into the house than the mother, one of whose daughters was a member of the church, said: "I am so glad you have come. We have been talking about it and we know we ought to join the church." The mother and two of the children made their decisions that night. Two other girls were not at home; other workers visited them. The result was that five members of that family united with the church as a result of the visit of the two Indian women.

Somewhere I have heard the story of a woman who kept a boardinghouse for medical students and who encouraged many

115

a young man to continue his premedical course when sorely tempted to quit. That may be fiction but there is also a true story of a woman who kept a boardinghouse not solely for the purpose of making money but principally for the purpose of getting close to people in order that she might win them for her Lord. The home may be an evangelistic agency.

Jesse M. Bader, secretary of evangelism of the Federal Council of Churches, tells the story of a couple in St. Louis, whose son had died. In their loneliness they telephoned the Y.M.C.A. to ask if there was staying there a young man far away from home who might enjoy a Sunday in their home. The "Y" sent them a delightful young fellow, whom they enjoyed so much that they decided to make the entertainment of young men a part of their regular Sunday program. Every Sunday the "Y" sent them a young man from the dormitory. Each young man met them at the morning service of their church. He was instructed to ask the usher to seat him in their pew. After the service he went home with them, and they would say as they showed him their son's room: "This is our boy's room, but he is away. It is yours for the day. Make yourself at home in it. We'll call you when dinner is ready." Sometime through the day they always made an opportunity to talk with their guest about his relation to Christ. They followed this custom for years, and many a young man accepted Christ in their home or soon after his Sunday visit there. At one time the host and hostess gave a dinner for the young men who had joined churches in St. Louis through their contact with them in their home. Of course hundreds of the men had gone to other cities, but of the men who had joined churches in St. Louis, four hundred, with their wives and children, sat down to dinner that night, a remarkable testimony to the evangelistic opportunities in one's own home.

But the influence of women is not confined to the home. Women engage in endless activities that present evangelistic opportunities. Although religion may not be taught in American public schools, the schoolteachers have a strategic op-

116

portunity for sharing their faith with boys and girls. Christian nurses are often closer to a patient than the patient's own family. Frequently they are the recipients of their patient's confidences. Often do they talk of the deeper things of life. What great opportunities are thus presented to those who are ready to witness for their Lord. Although I have frequently passed through Salt Lake City, it was not until recently that I made the trip through the grounds of the Mormon temple. The guide was a neatly dressed woman, perhaps sixty years of age. She bore strong and repeated testimony to Mormonism. She expressed many ideas that seemed fantastic to me, yet she spoke with conviction, and doubtless has influenced many persons in the parties she has conducted through the temple grounds. One asked one's self if a woman could speak such legends with such power, why do not thousands of our Christian women, having the true revelation of God in the New Testament, speak all the while the wonderful works of God and the saving power of Christ?

I have in mind that attractive little girl behind the counter in a department store in Louisville, Kentucky. A woman bought a pair of gloves from her, and when the sale had been made the girl politely asked: "Would you mind if I asked you a question?"

"Why no, of course not."

"Well it's this: Are you a Christian?"

"Yes," said the woman, "it happens that I am, but I am interested. Why do you ask?"

"Because I am a member of the Walnut Street Church, and down there we are taught to ask people that."

That isn't a hard question to ask. Anybody can ask it. But if the Christian churches had thousands of women presenting Christ in such a simple, informal way, men and women would be added daily to the churches.

What I said to men in the last chapter must be said with equal emphasis to women. If we are to lift the capstone to its rightful place in the arch, women must exert their influence to win all sorts of people—men, women, young people, chil-

117

dren, the humble, but especially those who are capable of influencing the thinking and living of the country, the career women, the professional women, newspaper women, radio broadcasters, authors, women in politics, and educators. Women sit behind typewriters in newspaper offices preparing copy that influences the thought of thousands. Time was when the newspaper served as a moral guide to the people. Today most newspapers have become great business enterprises run for profit and propaganda. If we could win for the Kingdom of God the columnists and editors, and influence them to turn their departments over to Christ, as Charles M. Sheldon for one week edited the Topeka *Capital* as he believed Jesus would have done, we could turn the tide in the United States and see mighty waves of righteousness again laving our shores. A single woman's voice over the radio is heard by millions, from the socialite in her Park Avenue apartment to the woman in her farm kitchen in North Dakota. What an influence for God and righteousness such a woman could be if she were an informal missionary of the gospel of Christ.

Women write many books. With shame must we admit that many of today's best sellers written by woman are an influence for evil, vice, and crime rather than for righteousness. If the pen is mightier than the sword, let us capture the penwomen for our Christ.

What cannot a consecrated woman do by a simple word or act? A man came to the United States from India. Naturally he made many contacts with American people and attended many social functions. At a reception a woman asked him if he was a Christian. When he replied in the negative she said: "You don't know what you are missing." He was unable to get away from that brief statement. It eventually led to his decision for Christ. He is now an educational leader in an important part of India. What woman is there who could not wish that she had spoken that simple sentence, or what woman would not have been eternally grateful for having spoken that word that changed the life of Charles Wesley, whose influence in the great evangelical awakening was second only to that of his illustrious brother.

Says James Burns, in *Revivals, Their Laws and Leaders*:

Lying ill in bed, he was attended by a woman of a deeply devout character, and to her there came an intense conviction that she ought to speak some words of comfort to him. Long she struggled against it, but at length, overpowered, she entered his room, and with an intense voice said: "In the name of Jesus of Nazareth, arise! Thou shalt be healed of all thy infirmities." Charles Wesley was, according to his own confession, composing himself to sleep. Suddenly the words, breaking in upon the silence around him, fell upon his ears with startling effect. "They struck me to the heart," he says. "I never heard words uttered with like solemnity. I sighed within myself and said, 'Oh, that Christ would thus speak to me!' " Suddenly the light dawned, his whole being seemed to be caught in a transport. From the lips of a woman without education, and driven by a mysterious and uncontrollable impulse, the message of deliverance came.[2]

Any woman may engage in conversation, write a letter, or give another person a New Testament. These are simple things, but they may prove momentous. Who would not give anything to have engaged in that conversation overheard by John Bunyan, written that letter received by Allen Gardiner, or handed a New Testament to Dostoevski!

"People will talk," is often a red signal hung across a questionable road. But as long as there are people, and as often as they get together, people will talk. What they talk about, and how they talk about it, is important. In his *Grace Abounding*, John Bunyan shows how valuable the right sort of conversation may be. Talk may be trivial or it may be transforming. Listen to Bunyan:

But upon a day the good providence of God did cast me to Bedford, to work on my calling; and, in one of the streets of that town I came where there were three or four poor women, sitting at a

[2] By permission of James Clarke & Co., Ltd.

door in the sun, and talking about the things of God; and being now willing to hear them discourse, I drew near to hear what they said. But I may say, I heard, but I understood not; for they were far above, out of my reach. Me thought they spake as if joy did make them speak; they spake with such pleasantness of Scripture language, and with such appearance of grace in all they said that they were to me as if they had found a new world, as if they were a people that dwelt alone, and were not to be reckoned amongst their neighbors.

Another day, as he was again passing by, the same poor women were still occupied with the same things of God. Adds Bunyan:

By these things my mind was now so turned that it lay like a horse-leech at the vein, and was still crying give, give. Yea, my mind was now so fixed on Eternity, and on the things of the kingdom of heaven, that neither pleasures, nor profits, nor persuasions, nor threats could loosen it, or make it let go its hold.

As the letter of a woman led to Allen Gardiner's conversion, the conversation of these women led to John Bunyan's conversion and gave us *Pilgrim's Progress* and *Grace Abounding*.

Nothing would have seemed more hopeless than the chance that a letter from a religious old lady would make an impression on a dashing young naval officer, yet Allen Gardiner always considered the receipt of that letter as the turning point in his life. In her letter she tells him that what he needs, above all else, is a new heart. "Remember," she says, "this is not my phrase; it is the very word of Scripture. And unless we have this new heart, this clean heart, this heart of flesh given in exchange for a heart of stone, we cannot believe effectually." She quotes from David: "Create in me a clean heart, O Lord," and from Ezekiel: "A new heart will I give you." "You will perhaps ask," she continues, "how this new heart can be obtained? It is the gift of God exclusively; none but he can create it. It is probable, dear Allen, that you and I will never meet again on earth; and, if not, let me hope that we shall meet in that place where all must hope to be, clothed in the Saviour's perfect righteousness."

That letter led to Allen Gardiner's conversion and further led him into the distinguished service he rendered the cause of missions.

It was a great day for the world when someone lent Shelley *Faerie Queene*, but a greater day when two women slipped a New Testament into the hand of Dostoevski, when he was on his way to imprisonment in Siberia. Taking advantage of a moment when the officer's back was turned they whispered to him to search it carefully at his leisure. Between the pages he found a twenty-five-ruble note. The money was a vast comfort to him, but the New Testament itself proved an infinitely vaster one. His daughter tells us that during his exile that Testament was his only solace:

He studied the precious volume from cover to cover, pondered every word, learned much of it by heart, and never forgot it. All his works are saturated with it. Throughout his life he would never be without his old prison Testament, the faithful friend that had consoled him in the darkest hours of his life. He always took it with him on his travels and kept it in a drawer of his writing table within reach of his hand. He consulted it in all the important moments of his life. It was his comfort in the hour of death.

Let no Christian woman say "I am an exception. I have no strength nor chance to help lift the capstone." Many and important indeed are the opportunities in evangelism open to consecrated women.

X

Chips Off Old Blocks

FLOOD WATERS SWIRLED under the bridge. The mad stream had risen almost to the point where a group of excited boys stood watching from the bank. The ice had broken up and great chunks floated past them.

"Look," cried a lad as he pointed to an unusually large cake of ice. As they followed the direction he pointed out, the boys saw a pile of wood on the ice. A rabbit was hopping around on the wood.

"I'm going to get him," the lad shouted over his shoulder to his companions, as he dashed down the bank where his boat was moored. He turned its bow into the flood and rowed out to the floating woodpile. He caught the rabbit, put it in his overalls pocket. On the way back the little boat was caught in a whirlpool and capsized. The lad disappeared from sight. When his body was recovered and laid on the riverbank, one of the lads thrust his hand into the dead boy's pocket and drew out the dead rabbit. Holding it up he said: "That's what he gave his life for."

A whole generation of modern young people seem to be frittering away their lives on things that seem to have as little value as that dead rabbit. "A cap and bells we buy with a whole soul's tasking." Even of some formerly earnest young people it must be said,

> Just for a handful of silver he left us,
> Just for a riband to stick in his coat.

Yet we cannot blame them too severely when we remember they are only chips off old blocks. They are children of frustrated parents whose idealism was blitzed into a heap of futility by World War II, the children of the violent emotions, the suffering, and the immoralities of war. Nazism, Communism, and other forms of totalitarianism, led some parents to believe that in those systems they had found a cause great enough to command their loyalty, even their lives. When Helmuth von Moltke was on trial for his life before the Nazi prosecutor Freisler, the issue—as von Moltke described it in his last letter to his wife—became simply one between a man whose views of life were Christian and the Nazi state. Freisler remarked: "Nazism has only one thing in common with Christianity: it also claims the whole body and soul of man."

Fired by idealism, youth must find the great cause. Its supreme moment comes when, like William Wilberforce, William Lloyd Garrison, or Abraham Lincoln, it enlists in an enterprise great enough to command its total personality and service. We may be sure that under the ashes of disillusionment youth's fires of idealism still wait to be stirred into a flame. Cruelly deceived by pseudo saviors and false utopias, present-day youth still yearns for the great adventure. We know that the supreme cause is the battle for God's Kingdom. The hope of the world, the one ideal worthy of our faith and worth our lives, is the Kingdom of God. The world revolution to put Jesus Christ upon the throne of world empire, and thus bring to mankind lasting love, justice, peace, and happiness is the supreme cause. To recruit men for that revolution is our supreme business. Someone once asked Lyman Beecher: "Mr. Beecher, you know a great many things. What do you count the greatest thing that a human being can be or do?" The famous thinker replied: "The greatest thing is not that one should be a scientist, important as that is; nor that one should be a statesman, vastly important as that is; nor even that one should be a theologian, immeasurably important as that is; but the greatest thing of all is for one human being to bring another to Christ Jesus the Saviour."

Julius Caesar gave his life for power; Cicero gave his life for praise; Mark Antony gave his life for pleasure; but General William Booth, founder of the Salvation Army, gave his life to reach men for Christ. Queen Victoria once asked

123

General Booth if there was anything she might do for him. Booth replied: "Your Majesty, the passion of some men is for fame and of others it is fortune, but my passion is for souls."

You and I may know that here is the great cause, but most of the world's young people do not know it. To give our American youth a vision of this great objective is exceedingly difficult. We are in part responsible for our sad dilemma. Most Protestants are grateful for the separation of church and state, but amid the blessings accruing to us from this arrangement there is also a staggering problem. We have separated religion from life, and we now see that democracy is dependent upon morality, and morality in turn is dependent upon religion. Christianity is an integral part of a well-rounded education, but generally speaking, in our public-school system teachers are naturally wary of mentioning religion. Consequently children and young people grow up with the idea that religion does not matter. It is divorced from life and not considered essential to a good personality. This conviction is often deepened in the minds of young people in our state-supported universities. Even in our so-called Christian colleges, established for the promotion of the faith, the difficulty of securing professors who combine sound faith and genuine scholarship offers little hope of solving the problem.

Our schools may be producing scholars but many of them are godless scholars. They inform the mind but do not discipline the spirit. The result is a sad deficiency of Christian character, the element that renders a nominally Christian nation strong and successful. What wonder life has become almost wholly secular!

Declares Charles Seymour, president of Yale:

It is a shame that a comparable development of spiritual power has not occurred to direct the instruments of physical power which science has suddenly placed in the hands of man. There is no field in which the vigorous and combined leadership of educational institutions at all levels is so sorely needed as in the spiritual."

Dave Boone, New York newspaper columnist, commented on Seymour's statement:

Mighty few people will deny that, but the country will probably slop along as usual, letting the public schools, prep schools, and colleges put almost everything ahead of spiritual values. It might help if the big colleges would limit their honorary degrees to men who have done big things in the world of faith. If any big colleges plan to honor men for achievements in the field of super-destructiveness and materialism this season, I suggest they scratch 'em and make some substitutes.

But the source of our difficulties lies even deeper than in our school system, if Julian Benda is to be believed. He affirms in his book *The Great Betrayal*, published in France in 1927, that the greatest betrayal of all history is the betrayal of the people by their public servants, the intellectual leaders of modern life. For the most part in the world's history, Benda believes, the intellectuals have been trustworthy. They have sought truth with more or less open minds, and they have taught the truth as they saw it. When they went astray they were generally corrected by their fellows.

But in modern times, Benda contends, the intellectuals have betrayed us. Historians have written history not in an unbiased way as faithful reporters of the facts as they are. They have rewritten history as propaganda. They have selected the facts that seemed to prove what they wanted them to prove, and have distorted the significance of events to bolster certain doctrines they desired to inculcate. Since the appearance of Benda's book Germany has provided a glaring example of this sad betrayal. German historians wrote to prove the doctrine of the superman—the superiority of the German people and the overlord state, the right of Germany to control the destinies of other nations, the will to power, the glory of war. Hitler went so far as to imprison those historians who refused to promote this betrayal.

J. Edgar Hoover insists that children and young people have been further betrayed by their parents. He has accused

American parents of a "form of treason" in their "betrayal of their trust through their failure to provide the loving guidance and devotion which are the endowment and birthright of every child."

Ministers of the gospel may share in guilt for the betrayal of youth as well as age. When a minister wrests Scripture from its context, when he selects from the Word of God only that which may promote a certain point of view or a certain theological party rather than preaching the whole counsel of God, he is betraying his people and the Kingdom of God. The only person worth listening to is the person who does not speak for a group or a party, nor according to the spirit of the times, who does not echo the popular formulas, who sees and understands the spirit of the times but does not surrender to it. To such a one young people will respond as four young Scots responded to Dwight L. Moody. These young Scots were very conscious of their superiority as cultured men, but spiritually they were extremely cold. They lived in the city of Glasgow and had organized themselves into an exclusive group called "The Plumes" (Scottish for plums). When they met they put their thumbs on the table and repeated a little ritual. Dwight L. Moody came to Glasgow. The Plumes felt it beneath their dignity to go to hear him. One said: "I understand he breaks the King's English in every sentence." Said another: "Yes, but I understand that he also breaks hearts."

Finally they condescended to attend one of Moody's meetings. The building was filled, and the four were ushered to seats in the very front, where they received the full impact of Moody's personality and message. They were brought under deep conviction and completely surrendered their lives to Christ. The contribution made by those four surrendered men to the progress of Christianity in the last generation is beyond human power to calculate. One of them was Henry Drummond. He launched a program of evangelistic work among college students, with the aim of reconciling science and religion, which spread throughout the English-speaking world. His monumental work *Natural Law in the Spiritual*

World proved the means of saving the faith of innumerable young men.

Another member of the group was Sir George Adam Smith, a great Bible scholar and influential theologian who published many books, including the *Historical Geography of the Holy Land*, and delivered the Lyman Beecher Lectures at Yale in 1901.

The third member was John Watson, popularly known by his pseudonym Ian Maclaren, the author of *Beside the Bonnie Brier Bush* and other stories of Scotch life equally dear to the world. He was the second member of the group to deliver the Lyman Beecher Lectures at Yale, later published under the title *The Cure of Souls*.

The fourth "Plume" was Donald McLeach, the famous medical missionary to China.

In our generation we must challege and enlist youth as Moody enlisted those men of rare ability, as A. T. Pierson, speaking at Princeton, enlisted a young man who seemed to have great difficulty in rising from his chair when Pierson asked those who wished to enlist for Christ to stand. He was a strong, athletic young fellow by the name of Robert E. Speer. At Cornell University a young man by the name of John R. Mott responded in the same way. Yet not many such young men are likely to be enlisted in that way today. Preaching does not reach them. Typically modern young people do not attend evangelistic meetings, nor does it do much good to invite them to attend. We must discover new approaches to them. Seven out of ten American young people attend no church or Sunday school. It will take more than noted speakers and clever topics to attract them. The visitation of adults is not likely to win them.

What can we do? The best means of winning young people is through other young people. Youth knows the excuses and problems of youth. They know their likes and dislikes. They know how to appeal to them, and with a little instruction they can effectively present the claims of Christ upon young lives. Yet in frankness it must be said that not even the young are likely to win youth in great numbers today by direct approach through argument or testimony. Testimony may come later. As a young woman said in a conference recently; "From where he stands there isn't enough in religion to interest the modern young pagan."

Even in his day Nathaniel Hawthorne saw this. In his immortal story *The Marble Faun* Donatello and Kenyon had just left a church. While inside they had been thrilled by the beautiful windows. As they looked back from the outside, Hawthorne tells us:

Nothing was visible but the merest outline of dusky shapes—without a gleam of beauty.

"All this," thought the sculptor, "is a most forcible emblem of the different aspect of religious truth and sacred story, as viewed from the warm interior of belief, or from its cold and dreary outside. Christian faith is a grand cathedral with divinely pictured windows. Standing without, you see no glory, nor can possibly imagine any; standing within, every ray of light reveals a harmony of unspeakable splendors."

The modern young pagan stands without and he sees no glory in religion. A way must be devised to get him at least somewhat inside so that his point of view may be changed. There must be a step between paganism and Christianity; some way must be found to partly initiate him. Fellowship may be the first step to bring the outsider somewhat within, that he may catch a glimpse of the beauty of the cathedral of faith and service. The group may provide the first degree in initiation. The pagan world into which Christianity first entered was not so deeply impressed at first by the philosophy of Christianity as by the fellowship of Christians. More things are wrought by friendship than this world dreams of. Jesus made friends with people as the first step in winning them to himself. He was known as "a friend of publicans and sinners." His approach to the woman at the well was first one of friendship. He extended his fellowship to the godless. Through his proffered friendship to Zacchaeus he won the formerly friendless man to himself and his cause.

Jesus used social occasions to win young men. He formed a team of those who first became his disciples. This team did little if any preaching, but it gave a demonstration of fraternity that drew others like a magnet. Christian young people may make their first approach to outsiders through social events, then through the testimony of their lives and their lips win them to their Lord. The report of one denomination on youth work includes the following:

Three nights of visitation are undertaken: (1) A visitation just to make friends; (2) a visitation for cultivation and to invite the new friends to a fellowship social; (3) a visitation to seek definite decisions for Christ. Visitors are prepared in advance for these different types of calling. Some of our youth groups have been transformed in one week end by the challenge of this approach.

Each loyal young person is asked to make it the purpose of his life to cultivate three unreached individuals and to try earnestly to win at least one of them. He is urged to write on a "My Purpose" card the names of these people for whom he will be responsible, and each month he makes a report to the president of his group concerning his progress. He seeks these young people out in school, or wherever they are, and makes friends with them first, if he is not acquainted with them already. Thus the element of friendship may be a first step toward winning a decision for Christ. Where these friends do not respond to an invitation to a Sunday-school class or to church, they are invited to a fellowship event sponsored by the youth fellowship group. There the value of Christian fellowship is demonstrated, and during the period of informal sharing at the close the young people who have invited them tell briefly of vital spiritual experiences. Some youth are more impressed by such testimonies from their friends than by formal evangelistic sermons. The young worker continues to sponsor his prospects, and when he feels that the time is ripe he appeals to them to become disciples also. Where the young people have launched this program youth are winning youth for Christ and bringing them into church membership.

Talented young people are being trained and sent to the local churches for a week end to launch this program. In West Virginia a week-end state training clinic was held. Thirty young people were taught by actual experience how to conduct such a program. Then sixteen clinics were set up in all sections of the state under these thirty leaders who went out in teams of two. Thus other young people were trained to conduct clinics. The ultimate goal was to get as many as possible in the local churches to cultivate and win three of the unreached by the use of the "My Purpose" card. A letter from a teen-age boy who had been in a week-end clinic tells of winning decisions from all three of the people he had listed on his card, and asks for another card so that he can "start on three more." These young people are encouraged to

put their imaginations and their muscles to work beautifying and improving their churches and their equipment, teaching children, leading club groups, serving as . . . members of gospel teams or cheer groups, giving sacrificially of money, time, and talent. Others have answered community needs with a new quality of dedication. Discipleship has "spilled over" into summer service projects, vacation church schools, discipleship caravans, deputation teams, and coaching clinics.

The group demonstrates Christianity in action. Young people are impatient with the slow, calculating deliberation of their elders, but action captivates them.

I once covered the state of Iowa in deputation work. We traveled by automobile. One morning in the road ahead of our car there appeared a little gopher. He had enough time to get away if he had made a run for it, but instead he sat up to make a survey. That was his mistake. After we had passed there was no gopher. There are times that demand action rather than deliberation. Such is our time. "The day of march has come." This is not the time to temporize. There is no time to be lost. The urgency of the cause should appeal to young people. They demand action. Unless they find it in Christianity they will dash past and look upon the church as a relic of a beautiful but effete past now outmoded. On the other hand they will follow leaders who move swiftly toward a clearly conceived goal, as young Mark followed Jesus.

Mark was probably the youngest disciple. It is not without significance that a word more frequently employed in his gospel than any of the others is the word "straightway." While other writers were impressed by other characteristics of the Lord, Mark, because he himself was a young man, was impressed by the fact that Jesus was a man of action. Great evangelists have won multitudes by their dash and fire. They made mistakes but they were men of action. When he was criticized for his kind of evangelism Moody said: "I like the way I'm doing it better than the way they are not doing it."

The appeal that reaches young people perhaps more effectively than any other is the appeal to Christian service. Jesus used this appeal with young men: "Follow me, and I will make you fishers of men." The call to enlist for Christ in the big business of soul winning will reach modern youth.

A young mother came into a pastor's study. She told him: "I said to my husband the other day, 'I want to join First Church.' He replied incredulously, 'You do! Why, that's exactly what I too want to do.'" The minister could scarcely believe his ears, for he remembered the recommendation written across the face of the prospect card in his files which bore the woman's name. In imagination he could see it: "Do not follow up further—Catholic influence too strong." But she was saying: "I have been a Catholic. Years ago I came to daily vacation Bible school here. I have never forgotten it, and now I am ready —we are ready, Pat and Dorothy and my husband and I—to join this church."

Little by little the story unfolded. Bob Osterly, tall, blond, high-school senior, had been challenged to teach a class of boys only a little younger than himself. The fact that they were looking to him for Christian leadership influenced this more or less conventional Christian lad to dedicate his life fully to

131

Christ. He felt the need of winning each of the lads to a commitment to his Lord. A talk with Pat O'Malley led him to a decision. Pat talked about this decision at home. The whole family was touched, and the pastor had the joyous privilege of welcoming the four members of the household into the membership of the church. Mrs. O'Malley went to work at once in the daily vacation Bible school, which, as a girl, she had attended.

A sense of achievement will keep young people at work for Christ. When her church launched a visitation campaign a young college girl said: "I'm coming this one night but that is all. Don't expect me again." She came back to the church after the evening of calling walking on air. She had won another young woman to Christ. Every Tuesday and Thursday night for four weeks she went out and she won more people to Christ than any other member of that church. Her mother was a member of a church in a distant city. When the daughter urged her to become an active member of her church in the city where she lived, she gave her some flimsy excuse for not joining. While a man and his wife were driving her to church she told them of her mother's excuse. The man said: "I think your mother is right. That was a valid excuse." Then she went to work on the man and his wife, neither of whom were members of the church. When the invitation was extended at the close of the service the next Sunday eleven people responded, seven of them persons to whom this girl had talked, among them her mother and the man and wife who had driven her to church.

It is important to remember that young people follow young leaders. Let us win the leaders. A group of young people in a certain church won the captain of their high-school basketball team, who was also the tennis champion of the state, one of the most popular young men in the school. Naturally the news spread like a prairie fire through the high school. The young people had also won the swimming star and the champion mile-runner. "The Three Champions" influenced the whole student body of the high school for Christ and the church.

132

XI

Millstones

A LITTLE COLORED BOY sat in the sunshine on the porch studying the face of the colored schoolteacher who boarded with his family. She was reading a book.

"Tell me what you're reading," he pleaded.

"Once upon a time," she told him, "there was an old, old man named Bluebeard."

She related the fascinating story, and the little boy—Richard Wright—forgot the porch, the sunshine, the teacher's face, everything, and "reality changed, the look of things altered, and the world became peopled with magical presences." The teacher could not foresee that day that she had changed a life and produced an author, any more than Anna Leonowens, when she became governess in the court of the king of Siam, with its cruel slavery, could anticipate that dramatic moment on the balcony years later, with Lady Son Klin looking down on her rows of kneeling slaves and saying: "I am wishful to be good like Harriet Beecher Stowe—I want never to buy human bodies again. I have no more slaves. I give freedom to all of you who have served me, you are free." Nor could she envisage that day when her pupil Prince Chulalongkorn would say: "If I live to reign over Siam I shall reign over a free and not an enslaved nation." Nor again could she see the reign of this same King Chulalongkorn and the schools established all over the kingdom, the missionaries who would come into Siam, and the hospitals and the churches that would spring up under his influence. If she could have seen all that, doubtless she would have rejoiced in the toil of those difficult years and been content.

One wonders how many of those who work in the church school, often amid discouragements and at the point of personal sacrifice, realize the strategic opportunity they have to mold impressionable children for the Kingdom of God. No one can measure the influence of faithful Sunday-school teachers and officers in the work of evangelism. Indeed our greatest hope for winning a world for our Lord is in winning boys and girls to him before they have adopted the pagan standards of the world around them. Again and again so-called educational evangelism has demonstrated its power to win and hold more people than any other method. A study was made in Ohio of a group of churches over a period of thirty-five years. In that thirty-five-year-period eighteen hundred evangelistic campaigns were held in those churches. At the end of that time those churches had five hundred less members than at the beginning of the period. The superintendent of one Methodist Sunday school, on the other hand, developed his teachers as personal soul winners. The Sunday school began the thirty-five-year period with an enrollment of one hundred. At the close of the period it had an enrollment of three thousand, and six thousand had been received into the membership of the church out of the membership of that Sunday school during the thirty-five-year period. Our Lord was known as a teacher. The New Testament leads us to suppose that he delivered few sermons. Most of his preciously short three years on earth were devoted to teaching. His followers were known as disciples, learners. In time they in turn became teachers. His last words to them were: "Make disciples . . . teaching them."

Jesus was especially solicitous regarding the welfare of children. He was in hearty accord with the Old Testament insistence regarding spiritual truth as a sacred trust committed to us by the fathers to be transmitted in turn to our children and our children's children. We are untrue to this trust, and we commit a crime against childhood, if we fail to teach them the way of life eternal. Jesus becomes severe regarding this matter. He says that it were better that a millstone were tied about our necks, and that we were drowned in the depth of the sea, than that we should offend one of these little ones.

How much our age has to answer for its crimes against children. In a "world they never made," they have been blown to bits in a hundred cities of the world, sold into slavery at the age of eight, hanged as spies, and subjected to every kind of anguish and humiliation. In Sicily we watch little old men, who prove to be children not yet in their teens, being herded into the sulphur mines. In Russia we watch the mass murders by the Nazis, with children always in the foreground, and see the young bodies drained of blood to give transfusions to wounded German soldiers.

The nations can never atone for such crimes against childhood, but the church must not commit the further crime of neglecting to teach children the great spiritual truths that will lead them to the Saviour. No one else will do it if our Sunday schools and churches fail. In our day we cannot rely upon the home, for again and again we have been told that 85 per cent of parents are liabilities rather than assets to their children. Our American public schools will not do it. A statement by an American denomination is in point:

General education deals with facts, knowledge, skills. Christian education deals with values. General teaching presents possibilities, alternatives, opportunities. Christian teaching guides decisions. The general teacher transmits ideas. The Christian teacher shares an experience. General education answers "What?" and "How?" Christian education answers "Why?" The world staggers and starves today because whole peoples have followed the wrong answer to the "Why?" of life. Christ has the right answer. He gives it through his teachers.

The truths of the Scripture and the Christian life are a sacred trust committed to us by faithful fathers and mothers in Israel. We are saved today because they led us in Christ's way. The coming generation can be saved only as we teach them and lead them.

For some years past the churches seem to have lost interest in teaching the young. Sunday schools languished. This may have indicated many things. In the days preceding World War II energy and optimism pulsated through various nations like

Germany, Italy, Japan, and Russia; but by way of contrast the United States seemed old, almost senile, devoid of a sense of mission and cursed with a defeatist attitude. The people no longer depended upon their own initiative. One of the evidences of the old age of the country was the enormous decline in the birth rate. One hundred thousand fewer boys and girls entered the first grade of our public schools each year. Under these conditions it was inevitable that our Sunday schools should decline in membership and attendance. The churches seemed too discouraged to put forth great efforts to teach children. Since Pearl Harbor, however, the United States has been invaded, not by a foreign army nor by an army of immigrants from foreign lands coming through Ellis Island, but by millions who have come to us through the gates of birth. This army presents a new day for the church school, a vast field of evangelism.

If evangelism is the capstone of the Christian temple, it is the most important business of the church school. If the capstone of the arch is missing, if the church school considers its task as that of developing boys and girls merely in ethical culture, if there is much concentration on the essential elements of modern pedagogy, but no effort to win the children for Christ and develop them in discipleship, the church school wholly misses the mark. The evangelistic purpose must motivate all Christian education, for judgment of the church school is eventually based upon its success in leading its pupils to become disciples of the great Teacher, learning of him, living by his precepts, and serving him in every area of life. The true teacher is an evangelist. Because the teachers know their pupils best and have time for the interpretation of Christ and the Christian life in class periods, they are the ones who can best win them. We must therefore be careful to secure true Christians as teachers of the young. A teacher must first know Christ personally before he can introduce others to him. Christ must have forgiven his sins and abundantly satisfied the deepest needs of his own life before he can recommend him to others. We must not have unsaved teachers in our church schools.

It was said of Rip Van Winkle: "He tried at farming—found

it rather slow; and then at teaching—what, he didn't know."
But that must not be true of the church-school teacher. Emerson defined a teacher as a life-sharer, not one who merely imparts information but one who shares his own points of view, feelings, aspirations, and satisfactions with those who sit before him. The pupil has a right to turn to the teacher and ask: "Sayest thou this thing of thyself, or did others tell it thee?" A teacher should have an understanding of the evangel and evangelism if he is to deal intelligently with his pupils. It is a sad thing when we see crippled people on the streets and realize that they will in all probability go through life maimed, possibly because of the ignorance or the blunders of nurses or physicians, but it is a sadder thing to realize that thousands of people may miss eternal life because some Sunday-school teachers have been careless or blundering in dealing with immortal souls. On the other hand, what satisfaction comes to teachers who see children growing up like sturdy oaks in Christian faith and service, and who realize that they were to them the voice of God calling them to himself; they planted the ideas that led them to Christ and developed the attitudes that made these young lives strong and useful in the Kingdom of God.

In *The Autobiography of William Allen White*, the sage of Emporia says:

My clearest memory of the Indians comes when I think of Temple Friend, a boy older than I, who as a baby about a year old had been kidnaped by the Indians—leaving his mother scalped and playing dead in an Indian raid in Texas.

. . . .

Time after time his grandfather, the Reverend John Friend, who had been a missionary to the Indians when the boy was taken, made a sad journey into the Indian nation looking for him. Of course, the government gave the grandfather every opportunity. Year after year he lined up the little boys of every tribe in a row and went down the line calling one word.

"Temple?" he would whisper gently, not to shock him. "Temple? Temple?"

137

But no boy responded. Still, year after year, for nine years the old preacher went down that line all over the Indian country where the reservation Indians were caged. One day he started down the line, softly intoning his everlasting question to a dozen boys standing beside a wall.

"Temple? Temple? Temple?"

And just as he got to the end of the line, as hope was sinking, one boy slapped his breast and cried out: "Me Temple!"[1]

Can you think of anything greater to be than the mouthpiece of the eternal God, calling his children to him and hearing one and another saying: "Hear am I, Lord. I hear thy welcome voice that calls me, Lord, to thee"?

It should be made plain to teachers that their main business is to lead their pupils to Christ. Well-prepared lessons for the Sunday school will not be haphazard or merely interesting or entertaining. They should be carefully planned to lead pupils step by step toward the greatest decision of their lives—that of accepting Christ as Lord and Saviour. In each age group the child should be confronted with those ideas and truths that his experience makes it possible to understand and his development makes essential to his growth toward his decision for Christ, so that when that decision is made it will be an intelligent decision and include an enlistment for Christ and participation in his church's program of missions and Christian service with which he has become familiar, to some extent at least, through the lessons he has learned in the church school.

It is as great a mistake to force premature decisions on children as it is to force premature development of plants and flowers. A superficial decision may inoculate the little child against a normal and thoroughgoing life decision involving the total program of Christianity. Rarely is a primary child ready to make this great commitment with understanding, but he can make many commitments to the way of Jesus that are a natural preparation for his later decisions; and after children have made the great decision for Christ, opportunities should

[1] Copyright 1946 by The Macmillan Company and used by permission.

138

be provided for the reaffirmation of faith during the successive stages of growth, that surrender may be kept up to date and its implications for the changed relationships and responsibilities of developing life be kept fresh and vivid.

We must therefore not conceive of evangelism in the Sunday school as a periodic effort but rather as a continuing process. Commitment to Christ is not an isolated act. The Sunday school must give boys and girls a clear understanding of who Jesus is and what it means to be a Christian. We must not consider Decision Day an extracurricular event unrelated to the week-to-week Sunday-school experience of the child. Nor can we brush our hands together after Decision Day and say: "Well, that's that. Decision Day is done—what next?" True evangelism in the Sunday school requires the continuous attention of the pastor and every officer and teacher in the school. It includes plowing, harrowing, seeding, cultivating, harvesting, and conserving. Childhood presents the most fertile and rewarding field for this spiritual activity, for children are much more responsive to the call and program of our Lord than are their elders.

It was some years ago that I visited a pottery on the Delaware River, but I have never forgotten the liquid clay that would take the form of any mold into which it was poured, the lumps of the same soft substance that might be molded with the hands, and then the clay that came out of the kilns so hard and settled in its form that it could be broken only by hammer blows. Too often churches wait until conversion must be brought about by some cataclysmic experience—if at all—instead of molding the clay of childhood into vessels fit for the Master's use in the early days when evangelism may be preventive rather than reformatory.

On an occasion when Dwight L. Moody was conducting meetings in a town in England, he returned home one night to the friend's house where he was staying. His friend said to him: "Well, how many were converted tonight in the meeting?"

"Two and a half," replied Moody.

"Why, what do you mean?" asked his friend. "Was it two adults and a child?"

"No," replied the evangelist, "it was two children and an adult. The children have given their lives to Christ in their youth, while the adult has come with half of his life." •

Christian workers are sometimes tempted to emphasize the importance of adults and minimize the promise in child conversion.

One summer I stood by the side of a little creek that flows out of a lake in northern Minnesota. A boy scout made it across the little stream in three quick jumps on the steppingstones in the water. If a person ignorant of the geography of the United States had stood there, he would never have suspected that anything of any importance would come of that tiny creek, for it is so inconspicuous, and, if its intended destination is taken into consideration, it does not start to flow in the right direction. Such judgment, however, would be hasty and immature, for that lake is Itasca, and the creek in question is the source of the "Father of Waters." From where one stood at the source he could not see the ongoing greatness of the Mississippi in its 2,470-mile course, the Twin Cities with their flour mills, Memphis and its teeming life, New Orleans and the mighty flood pouring into the Gulf of Mexico. From frequently unpromising beginnings one can seldom envisage the vast outcomes.

One day in the intermediate department of the Sunday school, when the pastor invited the boys and girls to confess Christ, Wilbur Chapman's teacher said to him, as he gave him a gentle push at the elbow: "Wilbur, I think you ought to go." In response to the solicitude of his teacher Wilbur "went forward." Another Sunday-school teacher went tremblingly into a shoe store to talk to Dwight Moody about making a decision for Christ. Neither of those teachers could foresee the multiplied thousands who, because of their faithfulness, would be won to eternal life through the inspired ministry of the world-renowned evangelists J. Wilbur Chapman and Dwight L. Moody. Nor could Ira D. Sankey, Moody's beloved colaborer, envisage the world-wide results of the simple act of laying his

140

hand upon the head of a little gypsy boy in an encampment near Epping Forest and saying: "The Lord make a preacher of you, my boy." The boy was Gipsy Smith, who preached the gospel and won thousands to Christ on every continent of the world.

How many times we miss our chance to win children to an intelligent decision for Christ. Only one out of five children who enroll in our Sunday schools is won for Christ while he is in the school. One other is subsequently won for Christ, but three out of five who come to us in Sunday school—the majority—do not become Christians. The church school had a chance with Thomas Edison and Henry Ford and lost them, thus losing mighty potential allies for Christianity. It had a chance at John Dillinger and lost its chance to help save the United States from a criminal. It had its chance to win Trotsky long before he initiated the Russian Revolution. If he had been won for Christ how different modern history might have been. The missionaries in South Africa had a chance to win Gandhi to Christ. What a marvelous influence for Christ he would have been in the India that adored and followed him. It is too late to help thousands who have gone through our Sunday schools unevangelized, but let us put forth every effort to see that we do not miss our opportunity with the boys and girls now in our schools, and that we gather in and win for our Lord and his Kingdom the millions of American boys and girls who are not now in Sunday schools or churches. We have our supreme chance in winning children, but if we miss it we have no assurance it will come again. If an impulse to accept Christ is not encouraged and not expressed it atrophies and may never return. The land is full of men and women who might have become our allies if the tide of interest in spiritual things had been taken at its flood.

Not many become Christians after they have reached adulthood. Half of the accessions to our churches are young people between eleven and twenty-one years of age. They are our hope, for they do not have to overcome ingrained unchristian habits and attitudes that have developed during years of godless living. While it is usually much easier to win children to Christ and his way of life than it is to win adults, childhood conversion may be a real and creative experience. A young couple came to the evening service at Tremont Temple Baptist Church in Boston one summer. They had traveled many miles to be present. The husband had just graduated from Princeton Theological Seminary, and the couple were about to begin their work together in their first church. I remembered the afternoon years ago, when I called on that little girl and her sister, and led them to a decision for Christ and the Christian life. At the time it seemed a more or less routine matter, just two little girls in a Christian home whose background almost ensured their becoming Christians and church members. But after the service that summer Sunday evening the young minister's wife told me: "That day you came to the house and led us to Christ was the greatest experience of my life."

While many a child reared in a Christian home has always loved the Lord and wanted to follow him, there should be a time when a definite decision for Christ is made and publicly registered. The child will have to rededicate himself again and again to the purpose to follow Jesus, but the time of declaration will stand out as a red-letter day in his experience. This might be considered our "confirmation" in the nonliturgical churches—the time when the child who has loved Jesus from his infancy confirms that love and loyalty in a public espousal of the cause of Christ. But there are millions of children being brought up in homes devoid of spiritual life, where they receive no impulse toward Christ, and are never taken to Sunday school or church. The church is responsible for them also. We shall never save the world by teaching only the children who come to our Sunday schools of their own accord. If we are content to remain within the walls of our church educational buildings we shall watch the United States grow increasingly pagan. The unchurched children are a responsibility, but they also present a vast opportunity. If they will not come to us, we must go to them.

A young man in our nation's capital noticed that few children living near his church came to Sunday school. He made a house-to-house canvass and told mothers he would call for their children Sunday mornings. Now he looks like the Pied Piper when he arrives at the door of the Sunday-school building, with twenty-five or thirty children with him. He is an evangelist, for the chances are that many of those children will be led to Christ if the teachers are faithful to their important task, as children were led to Christ by Sir George Williams, the founder of the Y.M.C.A. When Williams first came to London he spent his Sunday afternoons seeking children for the Sunday school. A friend of those years told how Williams would run up long flights of stairs, knock on the door, and when it was opened perhaps only six inches, put his foot in the doorway and ask: "Do you have any children?" If the answer was "Yes," he would persuade the parents to let them come to Sunday school. "Have them ready next Sunday and I will call for them," he would say as he made his way to the next tenement or flat. Later when Williams became a merchant prince, and had been knighted by Queen Victoria, he still spent his Sunday afternoons in the same way.

Perhaps it was because an unnatural father sent him out into the world to fend for himself at the tender age of eight that when he grew to manhood George W. Chipman became a mighty hunter of other unfortunate boys. It was his habit to rise early on Sunday mornings and go down along the Boston wharves hunting waifs. Many a lad was brought to Tremont Temple by Deacon Chipman. One morning he found a boy in a barrel, where he had probably slept all night.

"How old are you, Bub?" he asked.

"Eleven years old."

"What are you doing here?"

The boy surveyed the toes of his shoes. He spoke slowly. "Running away from home."

"What's your name?"

"Russell Conwell."

143

"Come with me," said the kindly deacon. "I'll show you where to go."

He took the boy by the hand and led him into Tremont Temple. There he found Christ, and there later he became the teacher of a Bible class of hundreds of men. Through the mists of that early Sunday morning Deacon Chipman could not possibly see Grace Baptist Temple in Philadelphia with its thousands of members, Temple University with its thousands of students, and two hospitals in Philadelphia with their thousands of patients, all founded by Russell H. Conwell. Nor could he see the thousands who would gather to hear the famous lecture "Acres of Diamonds" delivered by Conwell more than six thousand times.

There is no royal road to success in the church school. We have adopted approved techniques, but to a great extent success depends, as it always has, upon going out into the community to find and win the children. It is an easy excuse for negligence to say there are no children in our neighborhood whom we may reach.

At a summer conference a pastor related a visit he had made to his former charge, a church in the open country. He was surprised to find the Sunday school had an average attendance of only thirteen children. "There are no children around here any more," the people complained.

"What about the Wood family?" the pastor inquired.

"All grown up and married."

"Don't they have children?"

"Yes, Al lives down here a piece—he has five children. Ed is still living on the old place. He has three children. Sam is at the next farm. He has four children." There were twelve little Woods besides all the other families. What that church needed was not reforestation but the ability to see all the little trees that had grown up among the Woods. Their eyes had never been opened to the opportunities that lay all around their church.

Some churches should consider establishing branch or mission Sunday schools where they may reach unchurched children. The Sunday school attendance in a downtown city church had declined by 50 per cent. The dwellings around it had become rooming houses for adults who had no small children. Not more than ten blocks from the church, however, there was a neighborhood swarming with children, where no Christian work of any sort was being carried on. One of the Sunday-school workers called at the homes in this neighborhood and secured the co-operation of parents. A small store was secured and recreational activities were organized. The children began thronging into the new center to join the clubs and organizations. Christian people have not always recognized the evangelistic value of the playground. Bible instruction is essential, but true evangelism of children and youth must include opportunities for them to be "doers of the word, and not hearers only." Recreational activities present these opportunities where the one decision to follow Christ is related to many decisions to take Jesus' way in one's daily life and thus fix the habit of Christ-centered living. In many rural districts schoolhouses may be used on Sundays for gathering children and young people to hear the gospel of Christ, or children may be won for Christ and the church in city and rural homes.

A deacon of a small-town church, whose home was in the country near the town, realized that the children in the vicinity of his farm were not being ministered to by any religious group, so he gathered them into his home and organized a Sunday school. The group grew until the home was too small to house them. Then a small building was erected, which has since grown into a lovely white country church with some two hundred members, many of them the children who might have remained pagans if they had not been led to Christ in the deacon's home. Again the group has swarmed, and another church is in process of formation out of the second Sunday school established.

Last year a single Protestant denomination gathered more than ten thousand boys and girls into what they call "Bible Story Hours" in homes opened to them by their people. The story of Jesus was taught in five lessons, carefully prepared by the denominational leaders. A well-qualified leader was selected for each group. An effort was made to make each child want to know more about Christ, and when he seemed ready to make an intelligent decision to follow him he was encouraged to do so. An effort was also made to enroll in some church school every child who attended the Bible story hours.

One church gathered 140 children into fifteen homes, and as a result the Sunday school, with an average attendance of 180 before the effort, increased to an average attendance of 240. In addition the church discovered eighty unchurched homes and won two whole families to Christ and the church. The church had spent $37,000 to remodel the building, but the congregation and Sunday school soon overflowed the new facilities that were expected to provide for increased attendance for years to come.

If we are to lift the capstone to its rightful place in the main arch of the Christian temple, we must have the help of the church school. Every church school should plan its work around three major objectives: (1) to increase its enrollment; (2) to win each one enrolled to Christ; (3) to provide special training for discipleship and church membership.

XII

Milestones

PERHAPS YOU HAVE CAMPED near the foothills of the Rockies and said to yourself, as you retired the first night: "Tomorrow I will arise with the sun and climb that first near-by foothill." When rosy-fingered dawn peered over the peaks you set out. You walked an hour—two hours—and you seemed no nearer the foothills than when you started, and you said to yourself: "I did not realize the hills were so high nor so far away." Such is true evangelism. We may start with a narrow circumscribed conception of it, but as we draw nearer we begin to realize that it is more lofty and vast than first we had dreamed.

In his *Life of Henry Drummond*, Sir George Adam Smith tells us that when the revival under Moody in Edinburgh grew to large proportions, some of the meetings were addressed by other ministers and laymen. Smith says:

The emphasis of every speaker was very properly laid upon "decision for Christ." In their natural anxiety to make this duty appear as simple as possible, some of these speakers laboriously succeeded in exhausting it of all reality, and shut up their hearers to the baldest travesty of faith that was ever presented to hungry men. A young man who had not heard Moody, but who was awakened and anxious, listened for several evenings to these speakers. He saw them whittle away one after another of the essentials of faith, and call him to a reception of salvation in which there was neither conscience nor love nor any awe. In their extremity they likened the acceptance of Christ to the taking of a five-pound note offered you for nothing, or of a glass of water, or of an orange! The veil grew thinner and thinner between his eyes and the mystery which was beyond, till at last, at the touch of one of their grotesque parables, it tore, and—there was nothing behind. In this feeling he attended a meeting conducted by Mr. Moody himself.

Moody's gospel, which had its centre in the Atonement, was the gospel of an Incarnate Saviour; no mere voice, but hands and feet, with heart and brains behind, to cleanse the cities of their foulness, organize the helpless and the neglected, succour the fallen, and gather the friendless into families. We have forgotten how often Mr. Moody enforced the civic duties of our faith. Yet read again his addresses and articles of the time, and you will believe that in the seventies there was no preacher more civic or more practical among us.[1]

All great evangelism has been rich in content, emphasizing the whole counsel of God and calling men into lives of Christian service. A soldier enlists not in order to secure a uniform but in order to serve his country, and an enlistment for Christ is not merely an induction into a society but an acceptance of the whole missionary and service program of the Kingdom of God. The ineffectiveness of many of our churches is attributable in part at least to a superficial and unscriptural perversion of evangelism in sharp and tragic contrast with the message of great evangelists. Jonathan Edwards insisted upon a complete crucifixion of the human will as the ground of salvation, and Charles G. Finney said of his meetings:

Sinners were not encouraged to expect the Holy Ghost to convert them, while they were passive; and never told to wait God's time, but were taught, unequivocally, that their first and immediate duty was to submit themselves to God, to renounce their own will, their own way, and themselves, and instantly to deliver up all that they were, and all that they had, to their rightful owner, the Lord Jesus Christ.

One of Charles Dickens' characters used to break vacuously into conversations with the irrelevancy, "There are milestones on the London Road." But there is relevancy about the statement, There are milestones on the way of the cross. Although sign boards have replaced antiquated milestones on modern

[1] By permission of Harper & Brothers.

highways, how eagerly travelers watch these modern milestones as they speed toward their destination. Now we are a hundred miles away. Presently a sign says, "75 miles to Hometown." We are a long way from Christian maturity when we begin the Christian life, and we are a long way from a Christ-controlled community, but evangelism is a means of bringing us nearer.

The surrendered life opens channels for the reception and release of the redemptive energy of God upon all areas of life. William Douglas Mackenzie once said: "Evangelism is the only true regenerative of the human heart, the only real cleanser of the life of a nation." Such great sympathetic waves of religious sensibility as the evangelical awakening in England begin in a personal salvation "to everyone that believeth," but they issue in redemptive processes that may transform all areas of life. According to a much-quoted passage from the Old Testament, on the basis of repentant prayer God is willing not only to forgive our individual sins but also to heal our land. There is an abundance of historical evidence that the gospel is the power of God unto individual salvation and collective redemption. Before it the pagan schools of philosophy bowed their proud heads. It freed the slaves. It purified marriage. It exalted chastity. It saved innocent infants from death through neglect and barbarity. It improved the economic status of those who embraced it. It built hospitals and schools. It put an end to the offering of human sacrifices in England, to the drinking of the blood of their enemies on the part of the Scandinavian peoples, to cannibalism in Scotland. Indeed we owe our civilization to evangelism.

We are yet sunk enough. We are still like former savages on some jungle island only half civilized. We still live in the jungle, whose law governs the lives of most of the natives around us, while we ourselves are only half Christianized. Yet we must remember the pit from which we were dug and mark the progress already made as we contemplate the glorious future God has set before us. Such contemplation naturally presents a question as to the ultimate purpose of evangelism. Like the mountains, that question has a way of eluding us. We are conscious that we have never found the answer. It is greater than our poor human minds. It must coincide with God's purpose in redemption, and who can fully comprehend that? The Apostle Paul says: "We know not what we should pray for as we ought," so that the Spirit who knows the mind of God must bring our petitions before God in groanings that exceed the possibilities of human language. A grand and mysterious purpose allures, but our understanding of the possibilities of Christian experience, and our appreciation of the greatness and power of God's grace are too limited. What is the mind of the Spirit who prays for us? The New Testament tells us God had his eye upon us before the foundation of the world, for he had a vast purpose for his people. What then was the hope he had in calling us to himself? The grand purpose is that we may be conformed to the image of his Son. There could be no greater purpose than that men should reproduce Christ in perfect manhood like the manhood of the Master. We are the heirs of God, not merely in the sense of getting something from God but in the glorious sense of receiving Godhood and godly character into ourselves, that Christ might not be alone but that he might be the first-born among many brethren, all being one with the Father, as Christ was one with him. Nothing less than this then is the purpose of evangelism. If one Christ could do what Jesus Christ has done for the world, what could even a comparatively small company of really Christlike men do for the world? Do not misunderstand me. Christ is unique. There is not another, and there never will be another only-begotten Son of God. But it is the purpose of God to produce a company of Christlike men—men conformed to the image of his Son.

The Apostle Paul pictures the whole creation as awaiting the appearing of the sons of God. The Greek word for "waiting" has the sense of "watching eagerly with outstretched head." Creation is "waiting it out" until a new race appears, not the superman Nietzsche anticipated but men transformed by the grace and gospel of God. A creation crushed by a sense of futility is awaiting the day that only the gospel can bring, that day of which some of us can say with Alfred Noyes:

> We have not found it, but we feel it trembling
> Along the lines of our analysis now
> As once Columbus from the shores of Spain
> Felt the new continent.[1]

This new day can never come through the mere humanistic seeking of social values. All the gospel some men have is a new economic order. But a godless religion has produced little good. Social schemes that spurn the supernatural have never developed spiritual stamina. It is useless to hope for lasting reform apart from regeneration. History proves that reform has been related to revival. As Elton Trueblood insists, we cannot preserve the Christian ethic apart from Christian faith. Men must be reconciled to God before they can reconcile the disjointed and antagonistic elements in our world. They do not learn to love God through loving men. They learn to love men when they first learn to love God. There is little hope of evoking Christian attitudes and Christian behavior from hearts into which Christ has never found entrance. The motivation for Christian service is not native to our humanity. The desire to serve comes only when men have established contact with God, only when, like Sidney Lanier, they say:

> By so many roots as the marsh-grass
>   sends in the sod,
> I will heartily lay me a-hold on the
>   greatness of God.

Yet Lanier does not exactly state the need. Rather than laying hold on God, men must yield themselves to the flow of the greatness of God through them. Henry Drummond once said:

According to the first Law of Motion, every body continues in its state of rest, or of uniform motion in a straight line, except in

[1] From "The Torch Bearers" in *Collected Poems of Alfred Noyes.* By permission of J. B. Lippincott Co. and Wm. Blackwood & Sons, Ltd.

so far as it may be compelled by *impressed forces* to change that state. This is also a first law of Christianity. Every man's character remains as it is, or continues in the direction in which it is going, until it is compelled *by impressed forces* to change that state. Our failure has been the failure to put ourselves in the way of the impressed forces. There is a clay, and there is a Potter; we have tried to get the clay to mould the clay.

The Bible does not urge us to transform ourselves but to yield ourselves to the transforming power of God. "Be ye transformed by the *newing* of your mind." The Greek is stronger than our usual translation into the word "renewing." Renewing sounds like a process of renovating, repairing something old. Man needs instead a new mind. He needs what Madame Guyon called "a creative hour with God." To put it simply, and in the timeless language of our fathers, which is most timely, men need conversion, the new birth, before there can come the cosmic consciousness that Christ has given them "birth to brother all the souls on earth." Modern psychologists have found new terms to describe this need and this transforming experience, but the experience is old as the New Testament.

Nicodemus, a member of the Sanhedrin and a true son of Israel, was naturally interested in the Kingdom of God. He came to Jesus to discover what was his conception of the Kingdom and his program for the Kingdom. Nicodemus sought a far-reaching social program, but Jesus told him that he must be born again before he could even see the Kingdom. There Jesus stated the sharp difference between Judaism and Christianity and between humanism and Christianity—only changed men, converted men, can see, or understand, or really help to build the Kingdom of God. In New Testament times men who were born anew released into a morally decadent world a mighty stream of influence that transformed all life, individual and collective, and today the only possible approach to a better world is through regenerated individuals.

Thomas Chalmers spent years thundering against the iniquities of Napoleon and the grosser sorts of sin, but when he was called from the church he had been serving he said to his parishioners: "For the first eight years of my twelve with you I thundered away against crimes of every sort, but the interesting fact is that during the whole of that period I never once heard of any reformation being wrought among you. It was not until the free offer of forgiveness through the blood of Christ was urged upon you that I ever heard of those subordinate reformations which I made the ultimate object of my earlier ministry. You have taught me that to preach Jesus Christ is the only effective way of preaching morality, and the lesson which I have learned in your humble cottages I shall carry into a wider field."

To John it was impossible for anyone to come under the influence of Jesus and ever be the same again. Only Jesus could influence a hardfisted tax collector like Matthew to turn from the receipt of custom and forget money in service of his fellowmen. Only Jesus could influence a money-mad Zacchaeus to say: "Half of my goods I give to the poor; and if I have taken anything from any man by false accusation [and he knew he had or he would never have thought of it], I restore him fourfold."

The milestones of evangelism that mark the progressive way of God's invasion of the soul of man are also the milestones of humanity's progress. It is over this road that we have come thus far on our way out of savagery.

If it is true, as Jesus insisted, that no man can even see the Kingdom of God before he is born again, then it must follow that when a man is born again he should see the kingdom.

> Heaven doth with us as we with torches do;
> Not light them for themselves.[8]

In downtown Pittsburgh there once stood the old Bank of Pittsburgh. For long years it was a landmark in that great steel center. The bank closed in the last depression and failed to reopen. The building was finally demolished except for the

---

[8] *Measure for Measure.*

façade with its classic columns that still stands like one of those movie sets some of us have seen in Hollywood. Just a front with nothing behind; great iron gates open into a parking lot. True conversion is never a mere façade, a front to nothingness. The church was not intended to be a parking lot. The gates of new birth must not open upon nothingness but upon a thrilling new life of service. After he read Jacob Riis' book *How the Other Half Lives*, Theodore Roosevelt went at once and left his card in Riis' office. On the card he wrote: "Have read your book and have come to help." The newborn soul must respond to the Word of God with a soul-transforming desire for service, a complete self-giving like the young man of whom Charles G. Finney writes in his *Autobiography*:

> I had insisted much, in my instructions, upon entire consecration to God, giving up all to him, body and soul, and possessions, and everything, to be forever thereafter used for his glory, as a condition of acceptance with God. As was my custom in revivals, I made this as prominent as I well could. One day as I went into meeting, one of the lawyers with whom I had formed some acquaintance and who had been in deep anxiety of mind, I found waiting at the door of the church. As I went in he took out of his pocket a paper and handed me, remarking, "I deliver this to you as the servant of the Lord Jesus Christ." I put it in my pocket until after meeting. On examining it, I found it to be a quit-claim deed, made out in regular order and executed ready for delivery, in which he quit-claimed to the Lord Jesus Christ all ownership of himself and of everything he possessed. The deed was in due form, with all the peculiarities and formalities of such conveyances.

In his essay on William Wilberforce, Sir James Stephen says that there was "some secret spring of action on which his strength was altogether dependent." Well might Sir James wonder at the mystery of the man, a man who had to surmount high hurdles in order to succeed, a hunchback, a misshapen little creature, yet whom nature had graciously compensated with unusual resourcefulness and many talents, to which, as is so often the case with handicapped persons, was added good humor and through self-discipline a peculiar charm of manner

which made him welcome in all circles. His musical and elo-
cutionary gifts made people seek and enjoy his companionship.
To these qualities he added such earnestness and sincerity that
when he rose to plead the cause of the slaves he seemed like a
man inspired. When Boswell heard him speak he said: "I saw
a shrimp mount the table, but as I listened he grew and grew
until the shrimp became a whale!" His hearers declared that his
face, when pleading for the slave, was like the face of an angel.
What was the secret of the man, the "secret spring of action
on which his strength was altogether dependent"? Wilberforce
was a product of the great evangelical awakening. J. H. Overton, the historian, says: "It was not only evangelicals but evangelicalism that abolished the slave trade."

William Wilberforce was a smart young "man about town,"
a member of five of the most exclusive clubs of London. It was
said that "he could drink as deeply and gamble as suavely as
most young dandies in his set." The night life of London
claimed him. As a young man Wilberforce traveled with Isaac
Milner. They always carried some books to read on rainy days.
On one occasion they slipped into their luggage a copy of
Philip Doddridge's *Rise and Progress of Religion in the Soul*.
Wilberforce read it, and it ruined his peace of mind. It haunted
him sleeping and waking. "My sin!" he cried, "my sin, my sin,
my sin!" "God be merciful to me a sinner!" was the cry of
his heart. God heard his prayer, as he always hears that penitent prayer, and his prayer changed to a song—"What infinite
love that Christ should die to save such a sinner!"

The same age as William Pitt, he lay with him in the grass
under a great oak tree one day. That was the day Wilberforce
caught the vision of his life work, the emancipation of the
slaves, and for fifty years his life was completely given over to
his great purpose. It was through his efforts that the Emancipation Bill was signed. He considered this work his sacred
calling. He had recognized his stewardship to God in the giving of his life to God's uses and God's purpose for him; and,
as he had given his life to God, so he gave him his possessions
as well. In a year of depression he gave away $15,000 more

155

than he made. Of course he could not keep that up, but he eliminated all luxuries and lived very simply in order to be able to give all he could to God's work. Wilberforce was one

> Who at all times and everywhere gave
> His strength to the weak,
> His sympathy to the suffering,
> His substance to the poor,
> His heart to God.[4]

This was the spirit of the great evangelical awakening. John Wesley himself practiced rigid economy that he might give largely.

Not only did the awakening abolish the slave trade in England; it

pioneered popular education, humanized the prison system, established a world missionary movement, emancipated England's "industrial slaves," and raised up valiant leadership both in Trade Unionism and the Parliamentary Labor Movement—that awakening inspired also the modern philanthropic and social-service movement, which carried blessing not only to all sorts and conditions of men, but even to the lower creatures.[5]

Through the awakening there came to men, touched by the spirit of God, a realization of the wrongs suffered by the people and a conviction that the task of changing conditions was their own.

John Howard heard the call to reform the iniquitous English prison system. He traveled more than fifty thousand miles and spent $150,000 of his own fortune to correct the glaring abuses of this system that was connected with brutality, corruption, prostitution, and drunkenness. He shut himself up in foul dungeons that he might feel the sufferings of the prisoners,

[4] Inscription on the memorial figure to General Charles George Gordon, in St. Paul's Cathedral, London.

[5] *This Freedom—Whence?* by J. Wesley Bready. By permission of the American Tract Society.

and he died of jail fever in Russia; but he brought to the captives freedom from the criminal abuses they had suffered. Like Wilberforce, Howard believed that reform was a sacred calling. His time, talents, and possessions were administered as a stewardship committed to him by God. The same was true of Lord Shaftesbury. What Wilberforce was to the slaves and Howard to prisoners, Shaftesbury was to the "factory slaves" of England.

In the year of Waterloo, when fourteen, a student at Harrow School, Shaftesbury witnessed a pauper funeral wherein drunken pallbearers, trying to turn a corner, tumbled in a heap, the coffin crashing to earth and cracking. That spectacle was to the Emancipator of Industrial England what the auction of the Negro girl in New Orleans was to the Emancipator of America's slaves. There, before God, the young peer pledged his life to the uplift of the degraded and the oppressed.[6]

Lloyd George has said:

The movement which improved the conditions of the working classes, in wages, hours of labor, and otherwise, found most of its best officers and noncommissioned officers, in men trained in institutions which were the result of Methodism. I never realize the effect Methodism has had upon the national character so much as when I attend international congresses. It has given a different outlook to the British and American, from the outlook of Continentals. . . . John Wesley inaugurated a movement that gripped the soul of England, that deepened its spiritual instincts, trained them and uplifted them; and the result is that, when a great appeal is made either to England or to America, there is always the response, and it is due to the great religious revival of the eighteenth century.

It was because the spirit of life in Christ Jesus had freed him that Shaftesbury felt he owed it to the "factory slaves" of England to free them. When pressing in the House of Commons for the emancipation of women and children from "white

* *Ibid.*

157

slavery" in the mines and collieries of Britain, he declared: "I have been bold enough to undertake this task because I must regard the objects of it as being created, like ourselves, by the same Master, redeemed by the same Saviour, and destined to the same immortality."

In the United States permanent institutions had their inception in evangelistic movements. One of the American fruits of the Great Awakening was the separation of church and state, the churches passing from state support to self-support at this time.

Charles G. Finney's emphasis upon the service of God produced converts who became intensely practical in their Christianity. Out of his revivals grew great reform movements.

In 1839 under the ministry of Elder Knapp was started the Washington Temperance Movement. Knapp's revival enraged the saloonkeepers. Two men, Mitchell and Hawkins, were in his meeting one night. From the church they went to the saloon. The proprietor was cursing Elder Knapp. Mitchell turned on the man and said: "If you keep up this abuse any longer I will never drink another drop in your house, or anywhere else, as long as my name is Mitchell." He then and there pledged himself to total abstinence. Hawkins and others joined him in the pledge. The movement that resulted was responsible for the reformation of tens of thousands of drunkards.

Going all the way with Jesus, as we follow him milestone by milestone through the New Testament, is one of the greatest recommendations of our gospel. When we have gone only the first mile in evangelism men are likely to question our motives and point out the disparity between the one who opened the eyes of the blind, healed the sick, and ministered to prisoners, the poor, and needy, and his professed followers of whom he once said: "The works that I do shall he do also; and greater works than these shall he do; because I go unto my Father." The church must make the influence of Christ felt in every realm of human life through redeemed men. Certainly this is part of evangelism.

It is not the business of the church to find the solution of all

the manifold economic, social, and political problems that vex
the world, or to discover techniques in these various realms,
but to provide an inspiration through the incoming of Christ
into individual lives and the infusion of new spiritual life into
the community. When men are energized by the spirit of
God they find their way, and they become irresistible in their
passionate espousal of the good of their fellows.

When the spiritual tide is low in the church the people lose
their spirit of service in worldly selfishness. They do not care
for the poor and neglected. They are indifferent to the evils
that flourish within a stone's throw of the church. When, however, the tide comes in, their ships come in with the tide. Spirit-
ualized Christians begin to think of themselves as their brothers'
keepers and on their part the poor receive an infusion of new
stamina so that they improve their own status. When the capstone of evangelism rises to its place those who enter into its
exaltation rise with it. Even those who were formerly a menace
to the state become profitable to it. Evangelism is then a vast
program, all the implications of which we may not comprehend,
but the revealed responsibilities of which are great enough to
demand the full allegiance and effort of every person who
truly cares for the Kingdom of God.

XIII

Completing the Arch

THE PULLMAN CONDUCTOR for whom Polish Catholic Tony had worked for some years was surprised one Sunday when Tony announced he was going to accompany him to church. At the close of the service he was still more surprised to see Tony at the back of the church shaking hands with the people as though he had known them for years. On the way home Tony said: "Your church, good place, everybody good feeling. Everybody loving Jesus. Everybody shaking hands wid Tony. My church, no one good feeling. No one loving Jesus. No one shaking hands wid Tony."

Loving fellowship is the atmosphere which both attracts outsiders and in which spiritual babes develop into full grown men and women in Christ. What the sun means to the growth of flowers the atmosphere of love means to little children in the home. They learn to walk through the encouragement of loving parents. So young Christians learn to walk in the atmosphere of fellowship. To receive converts warm with the love of Christ into some cold churches would be like trying to raise chicks in a refrigerator instead of a brooder. Or to return to a figure frequently employed in this volume, if there is to be a transfusion of spiritual life the blood to be shared with another must be of body temperature. It must be clean and it must be the right type. Evangelism cleanses and warms a church, and while the love of the church members helps new converts to grow, the joy of the converts also overflows to the older members of the church.

An evangelistic church is always a joyous church. There is joy in the hearts of all those who have had a burden of sin and who know that their sins are forgiven and they are right with

160

God. R. W. Dale once said of the effect of the Moody and Sankey meetings in Birmingham:

I hardly know how to describe the change which has passed over them (i.e., the members of his church). It is like the change which comes upon a landscape where clouds which have been hanging over it for hours suddenly vanish, and the sunlight seems to fill both heaven and earth. There is a joyousness and elasticity of spirit, and a hopefulness, which have completely transformed them.

An evangelistic church where people are constantly being won for Christ will be characterized by a stimulating sense of achievement and love between those who are being won and those who are winning them.

A young man gripped his father's arm in church one Sunday morning when a young couple responded to the invitation. "Eleanor and I called on them this week," he said triumphantly. There is always joy in doing the Master's work and a thrill when we see the fruits of our labors. A woman who had just started to come to church with her family said: "This is what we have been missing all these years. You don't know what a difference it has made in our lives." There are thousands like that.

Everybody wants to be happy. Everybody wants to belong to a company of victorious people. Everybody naturally desires association with others of kindred minds. Such association promotes growth and growth is essential to spiritual health. While conversion makes us children of God it does not at once produce full-grown Christians. Speaking of God's deliverance from Egypt, Moses said to the children of Israel: "He brought us out from thence, that he might bring us in, to give us the land which he sware unto our fathers." The purpose of the church in bringing people out of sin is to bring them into the fullness of Christian life and experience. It is tragic when the church leaves converts to wander in a wilderness of immaturity, brought out but not brought into a land of beauty and blessedness. Converts may truthfully say: "Beloved, now are we the sons of God, and it doth not yet appear what we shall be."

Available to them are all the exhaustless resources through which Christian growth takes place, and before them lie the limitless possibilities of the Christian life, and yet many a church implies by its failure to nurture converts that conversion is a terminus rather than a point of departure. Indeed our record in this vitally important part of our Christian task represents the weakest and most vulnerable link in present-day Protestant strategy. That is probably because an evangelism that merely catches costs much less than an evangelism that both catches and holds.

In his book *The Effective Evangelist* Lionel Fletcher says:

When a baby is born into a house where it finds a welcome, everything possible is done for its comfort. If it is sick, the house is full of anxiety; when it laughs and crows, every member of the household smiles in sympathy. When it cuts its first tooth, there is subdued excitement. When it says its first word, all know about it and exclaim with pleasure. All want to help its baby feet to walk, and its every doing is narrated and rejoiced over. Its future schooling is planned long ahead, and the possibility of certain professions is kept in view years before it gives any indication of scholarship.

Yet by way of contrast the church often rejoices in the birth of souls and then neglects the babes in Christ.

A pastor who had made a number of calls on a man to get him to accept Christ and unite with his church pressed the man for immediate decision one day. The man said: "I'll tell you frankly why I have held back. I like you. I enjoy visiting with you and I know if I yield and join your church you won't come to see and talk with me as you have." He expressed a conviction that is unfortunately true in many cases. Like some physicians who show intense interest in persons extremely ill but who seem to lose interest when they are well on the road to recovery, we sometimes compass land and sea to win a convert but when he has been received into the church we seem to lose interest in his further development.

In a home I visit frequently there is a lovely painting of fields covered with snow and a very red barn in the background. In the foreground a hunter is tramping through the snow proudly holding up a rabbit he has shot and which he is evidently bringing home to prepare for the table. Who would think of whipping up a stream for trout, and then emptying his creel on the grass and leaving there the fish he had so proudly caught, or bringing down a deer, and leaving his game after he had spent long hours tracking it down? Yet poor Thomas Shepard, influential in helping establish Harvard, mourned, "I roasted not that which I took in hunting." Our Lord took pains to make his purpose crystal-clear in giving the great commission. According to this manifesto evangelism is not to be an isolated act of leading men to a decision but a process that involves the more sustained and conclusive effort of preaching the gospel, baptizing converts, and teaching them with the purpose of presenting them full-grown men and women in Christ.

In one great American church the altar was crowded with those who had "come forward" to accept Christ. One of the deacons said to a fellow deacon: "This is one of the greatest nights in our history."

"I am sorry I cannot agree with you," the second deacon replied. "To me it is a sad night because we have made no plans to help these people get started in living the Christian life."

T. C. Bau, general secretary of the Chekiang-Shanghai Baptist Convention, would agree with the second deacon. "It is relatively easy," he says, "for a persuasive missionary to lead an ignorant Chinese Buddhist to say he accepts Christ." To guard against the danger that Buddha is merely replaced by Christ, with no basic transformation of religious belief, the Chinese church sets up strenuous requirements for admission to membership. A person must attend church for six months and take a course of six or eight lessons with the pastor before he may apply for membership. Then there is a check-up to see what changes have been made in his life. If there are no changes he must wait. "With this method," says Bau, "if we take in twenty-five members in a year we know we can count on them."

We dare not evangelize people in a day and then turn them loose to take care of themselves. When they have been led to make a decision for Christ our responsibility has but begun. We are the ones through whom the great Teacher does his work. No true teacher would quit when he had done no more than enrolled his pupils. That is but the beginning, not the end of the educational experience. These people have become disciples, that is learners.

Now a process of teaching must be started. We have opened the portals of the church to them; now let us begin a careful process of instruction in the principles, purposes, and practices of the Kingdom. When Jesus called his first disciples he devoted three years to their training. The church of Christ must set aside at least some time for the training of new Christians. Each should be personally interviewed in his home by the pastor, and a five- or six-weeks training course provided. The leader of this group should study to present the basic truths of salvation and Christian living in such a simple, clear way that even children can grasp them. They understand the meaning of discipleship when it is properly presented.

A departmental superintendent was concerned lest a little girl in one of her classes had been received into the church without sufficient instruction. "What could a child of her age understand about the Christian life?" she asked. But her fears were allayed when she asked certain questions about the Christian life in the department. The little girl who had joined the church was the only member of the department who could answer the questions, and she answered them all to the complete satisfaction of the superintendent. She had been in the class in preparation for church membership. In this class the leader had made clear what it means to be a Christian, what our Lord did for us on the cross, what repentance and conversion mean, and the need of public confession. He had told the children how the church was organized, what its purpose is, and how it functions. He had made clear the doctrines and polity of the particular denomination with which they were affiliating. The sacraments or ordinances of the church and their significance were fully explained. Then the means of spiritual growth were described to the children. After such a course no one can say children do not know what they are doing when they unite with the church.

We need a quantitative development of Christianity, but perhaps one of the best ways to get that is to strive for a qualitative development. Henry Drummond once said: "To secure ten men of an improved type would be better than if we had ten thousand more of the average Christians scattered over the world." Long before Drummond, Gideon learned that a reduced number of wholehearted followers will accomplish more than a mixed multitude of halfhearted people. As a man said in a letter to me: "We fill our churches with unregenerate people, and then the ministers spend their efforts trying to get a dead army to fight and to be interested in prayer meetings and Christian programs."

The moral and ethical standards upon which John Wesley insisted helped make the great evangelical awakening a mighty force. The church of the present day must put more moral content into its evangelistic message and its training program. It must lift the standards of church membership. Better Christians will doubtless mean more Christians.

A college professor presented himself for membership in one of our churches. When called upon to give a testimony before the board of deacons he said: "I have lived in this city a number of years. I have watched the people of this church what they did and didn't do, and I have decided I want to live as you do. I want to do the things you do and not do the things you don't do, and I have accepted Christ and want to unite with the church."

There are many ways of culturing and cultivating converts. May I suggest a program successfully followed by at least one church? This church registers everyone who attends, whether they are members and have attended a thousand of this church's services before, or whether they are visitors attending for the first time. The card contains the question: "Are you interested in becoming a member of this church?" Many of these cards are signed in the affirmative. But perhaps because the answer to the question does not commit them to a definite decision to unite with the church then and there, although the invitation is extended at practically every service in that church, few of those who express their interest in uniting with the church come forward in the same service to offer themselves for membership.

The pastor considers it his most important responsibility to call upon all these people within the week. The church has an active evangelistic committee. The members of this committee visit outsiders who have signed cards but have not specifically indicated their interest in uniting with the church, but experience has convinced the pastor that calling on new members must be his personal responsibility.

After a friendly greeting and a discussion of the need of getting one's roots into the soil of the community where one has come to live, the pastor says to those who are already Christians and church members: "It will do you no particular harm to come forward in response to the invitation at the church service but it may be of immense help to others who are hesitant about declaring themselves for Christ. Your example may move them to action. Will you therefore come forward next Sunday when the invitation is given?" A pastor can preach with assurance and a note of expectancy in his tone when he is assured that a number of persons will respond to the invitation at the close of his sermon.

The average church might as well take out the front seats for usually no one occupies them. The church of which I write, however, is usually filled, yet whenever it is possible the front row of seats is reserved for the people who will come forward in response to the invitation. They are not asked to kneel nor to be conspicuous by standing during the closing moments of the service. They are greeted by the pastor and then seated in

166

the front row. The pastor believes that Jesus asks people to confess him before men but nowhere encourages his ministers to embarrass people before men. The pastor insists that those who plan to unite with the church on profession of faith meet him in his study for a personal conference before being welcomed into membership. He confers with each individual rather than meet the candidates in a group. In the conference he discusses the meaning of the step they are about to take, what it means to be a Christian and a church member.

The following appointment card helps new members keep the steps into church membership and the time for each step clearly in mind.

APPOINTMENT CARD FOR NEW MEMBERS

The Pastor will call at my home—
Date ....Hour ....

My appointment to meet with the Board of Deacons will be—
Date ....Hour ....

My appointment to be present at the Midweek Prayer Meeting to be voted into the Church will be—
Date ....Hour ....

My appointment for Baptism will be—
Date ....Hour ....

I will meet beforehand with the Pastor for instructions—
Date ....Hour ....

My appointment for receiving the Hand of Fellowship on Communion Sunday will be—
Date ....Hour ....

In most of our churches those who apply for membership are required to meet the deacons, the session, or the prudential or membership committee. This body, whatever designation it bears, should discuss with prospective members the church in

MEMBERSHIP ENLISTMENT

NAME ....

1. I was baptized in the ....Church of ....Date ....

2. Before joining this church I belonged to ....

3. I joined here by .... baptism ..... letter ..... experience.
   Date......................

4. I was born..............Wedding anniversary..............

5. I have held the following offices in the church..............

6. I have participated in church activities in these other ways
   ....

7. Other members of my family. Name, address, relationship, age
   group ....

WORSHIP AND ATTENDANCE

I shall nurture my Christian life and support the church by private and public worship.

I have read the Church Covenant and shall be guided by its spirit.

I shall make it my practice to engage in:

Daily prayer and Bible reading:
....Have daily devotions   ....Read a missionary magazine
....Use a devotional guide   ....Read the church paper

Weekly attendance at least one service of worship:
....Morning ....Evening ....Midweek

Regular attendance at a class or activity of my own age or interest group:
....Church School (Class ....)
....Women's Society ....Boy's Club   ....Youth Group
....Men's Club   ....Girl's Club   ....Parent's Club

general and in particular the church into whose membership they are being inducted. The committee should tell the newcomers about the work of the church, the budget, the missionary work, and giving to missions. There are many types of questionnaires like the one reproduced on the opposite page that may be used with persons being received into the church.

Each person is given a subscription to the parish paper, a devotional booklet, and a *New Member's Guide*. Each new member should be handed a pledge card, on which to make a financial pledge to the church, together with a stamped, self-addressed envelope in which to mail his pledge to the church office.

In one church there are three members of the church placement committee on the membership committee. It is now time for this committee to get into action. It is their responsibility to see that each new member is assigned to a sponsor or big brother or sister. An effort is made to select sponsors who come from the same state or section of the country as that from which their special charges also came. It is the committee's duty to see that each new member gets into the Sunday-school class, young people's group, or other organization in the church, for which he is best suited and which will be likely to be most helpful to him.

The responsibility of continuing to visit him in his home is now shared by the visitation committee of the church. The registration of all members at all services makes it possible to keep a careful check on new members. When it is discovered that a person recently received into the church has absented himself from services or is growing careless his sponsor is promptly notified and he visits him in his home.

The questionnaire makes it comparatively easy for the placement committee to enlist the newcomer in the sort of church work for which he is best suited and prepared. As soon as a member is received into the church the minister calls and presents a card such as is shown on the following page.

169

Welcome...

NEW TREMONT TEMPLE MEMBER

Believing that the following suggestions for Christian living should be kept to the glory of God and for the sake of a stronger and more consistent Christian life, I agree to the following:

I purpose to maintain a regular time of daily personal devotions, using the Scriptures and engaging in prayer, that I may grow spiritually. ☐

Believing that I need to be more fully instructed concerning the Word of God, I purpose to be a member of a Bible Class and faithfully attend Bible School each Sunday. ☐

Believing in the worth of a deep experience of worship, it is my purpose to be found in the Temple each Sunday morning and worship my Lord. ☐

With a vision of the opportunity of soul winning, I purpose to regularly attend the evening preaching service and whenever possible bring someone with me who has never made his definite commitment to Christ as Lord and Saviour. I will pray throughout the service that my guest will make a decision for Christ. ☐

Believing in the power and the necessity of prayer, I will faithfully attend the mid-week hour of prayer, and pray for the spiritual power of Tremont Temple that her ministry may be effective for Christ. ☐

Believing in the meaning of the family altar in a home, I purpose to maintain a regular time for family worship that my home may have for its foundation Jesus Christ and all of the heritage He has given those who follow Him. ☐

Believing in the worth of an eternal soul, I purpose to keep a prayer list of names of those who have never received Christ as their Saviour, and trusting in Him for guidance and wisdom, I shall endeavor to lead each one to Christ. ☐

Trusting in the Lord Jesus Christ for strength, I purpose to find a higher plane of Christian living that through my conversation, my personal habits, my manner and my attitude I may reveal Jesus Christ more fully in my life. ☐

Signed ....

The idea is not just to get the card signed, nor to leave it with the new member, but to make it the basis of a helpful conversation in which the minister may expound "unto him the way of God more perfectly."

The true pastor's work is never done. As Christian living is a ceaseless becoming, so the shepherding of souls is a task only completed when they enter the heavenly fold.

One morning as we drove through Montana I saw a shepherd ride across the fields to a sheep and her little lamb that had become separated from the flock. He tried to bring them back. Every now and then they would stop and he would have to go around them and urge them on. The shepherd of souls must never let his people stop. When they pause in the way he must be there to urge them on. "The saints are the sinners who kept on trying," said Robert Louis Stevenson. They are those who did not stop when they passed the first milestone, as Pilgrim did not stop at the cross just beyond the wicket gate. The Christian life is an extended series of new decisions, new levels, new quests, new vistas, new challenges, new attainments. There is ever an inner voice whispering: "Rise up, for this is not thy rest. Press toward the mark." If the shepherd of souls must never let his people stop, neither may he stop in his effort to win men for his Lord and build them up in our most holy faith. Jesus said: "I must work." The gods of the heathen banqueted, reveled, and fought; they did not work. But the Creator God "worketh even until now," and his servants must work. Neither education nor genius can take the place of work. George Bernard Shaw says a genius is a person who sees deeper than other people, and "has energy enough to give effect to this extra vision."

A man visited the locality from which Mark Twain came and about which he wrote.

"Did you know Mark Twain?" he asked a native.

"Sure."

"Do you know the stories he wrote and the people he wrote about?"

"Sure, I knowed all he knowed. The only difference between him and me is he wrote 'em."

A card in a Chicago restaurant said: "What a man knows has to be put into action to really count," and long years ago Jesus said: "If ye know these things, happy are ye if ye do them."

In an old hatbox in an antique shop in Wisconsin a young woman from California found a newspaper dated 1883. In it was the story of a woman who arrived at a church late for an "experience meeting."

"Oh, is it all done!" she exclaimed.

"No," replied the minister. "It is all said but yet much remains to be done."

Not all has been said in this book that might have been said, but the book will be a failure unless those who read it begin to put some of its suggestions into practice.

The national president of a denominational young people's organization described its evangelistic program to a group of youth.

"It is wonderful," they said.

"Yes, it's great," she replied. "Now let's do it."

Suddenly brought down to earth the young people said: "Oh, we didn't expect we'd have to do it."

A young minister read one of my books. He said: "It seems like a good book but the way to find out is to put it to the test." It had been a long time since his little church had received a new member. He followed the suggestions, as a good cook might follow the recipes in a cookbook, and on Easter Sunday he received forty new members.

While we need to improve our methods through reading and study, we also need to put into practice the simple techniques we already know how to employ. Just before I was introduced to speak at a breakfast of several hundred young people a solo was announced. A young man in the rear of the dining hall responded: "Miss Wait can't sing now; she's practicing." We frequently miss our opportunities for real service because we spend too much of our valuable time practicing, getting ready to serve, instead of putting to good use the things we already know how to do.

The laconic reply of Dwight L. Moody to Reuben A. Torrey, in answer to the question of how to begin, is always in point: "Go at it." When we do "go at it" the reward comes both in inner satisfaction and in tangible results.

CPSIA information can be obtained
at www.ICGtesting.com
Printed in the USA
BVHW040303270321
603431BV00009B/760